THE
WORLD
OF
MUSICAL
SOUND

Roderick D. Gordon

Southern Illinois University
Carbondale, Illinois

KENDALL/HUNT PUBLISHING COMPANY
2460 Kerper Boulevard, Dubuque, Iowa 52001

B   402078   01

Contents

Preface   vii

Acknowledgments   ix

Chapter 1   The Nature of Sound   1

   1.1   Definition of Sound, **1**
   1.2   Perceptible Frequency Range, **1**
   1.3   Musical Sounds and Noise, **1**
   1.4   Propagation or Transmission of Sound, **2**
   1.5   The Sine Wave, **2**
   1.6   Simple Graphic Construction of the Sine Wave, **3**
   1.7   The Audio Oscillator, **3**
   1.8   Physical and Psychological Parameters of Tone, **4**
   1.9   The Velocity of Sound, **4**
   1.10 Velocity of Sound in Air, **5**
   1.11 Reflection of Sound from a Plane Surface, **5**
   1.12 Reflection from the Parabola and Ellipse, **6**
   1.13 Refraction of Sound, **8**
   1.14 Diffraction of Sound, **9**
   1.15 Doppler Effect, **9**

Chapter 2   The Harmonic, Partial, Overtone and Inharmonic   13

   2.1   Definition of Harmonic, Partial, Overtone and Inharmonic, **13**
   2.2   Pitches of the Tones of the Partial or Harmonic Series, **13**

Chapter 3   Musical Scales   17

   3.1   Musical Intervals, **17**
   3.2   Muscial Scales, **17**
   3.3   Pitch Octave Identification, **19**
   3.4   Pythagorean Scale, **21**
   3.5   The Just Scale, or The Scale of Ptolemy, c. 130A.D., **22**
   3.6   Tempered Scale, **23**
   3.7   Cents, **23**

3.8   Other Tempered Scales, **24**
3.9   Tendency Tones or Pitches, **24**
3.10   Instruments Employing Tempered Intonation, **24**
3.11   Tuning Just Intonation, **28**
3.12   Tuning the Tempered Instruments, **28**

Chapter 4   Tone Quality   **31**

4.1   Complex Waves, **31**
4.2   Phase, **34**
4.3   Interference and Reinforcement, **35**
4.4   Effect of Phase on Tone Quality, **35**
4.5   Resonance, **35**
4.6   Sympathetic Vibrations, **36**
4.7   Formant Resonance, **36**
4.8   Aural Analysis of Complex Tones, **37**
4.9   Scientific Analysis of Tone Quality, **37**
4.10   Noise, **38**

Chapter 5   Beats and Combination Tones   **41**

5.1   Definition of a Beat, **41**
5.2   The Beat Tone, **41**
5.3   Practical Uses for Beats, **42**

Chapter 6   Stringed Musical Instruments   **43**

6.1   The Evolution of Stringed Instruments, **43**
6.2   Law of Vibrating Strings, **47**
6.3   Construction of Strings, **48**
6.4   The Bow, **49**
6.5   Producing the Tone, **49**
6.6   The Mute, **50**
6.7   Playing Harmonics, **50**
6.8   Tuning the Orchestral Strings, **52**
6.9   Construction Materials, **52**
6.10   The Evolution of Keyboard Stringed Instruments, **53**
6.11   The Piano, **54**
6.12   Piano Hammers and Dampers, **54**
6.13   The Piano Strings, **55**
6.14   The Piano Frame, **56**
6.15   The Piano Pedal Mechanism, **57**
6.16   The Piano Body, **57**
6.17   Tuning the Equally-tempered Instruments, **57**
6.18   The Acoustic Guitar, **59**
6.19   The Electric Guitar, **59**

6.20   Tuning the Strummed Instruments, **60**
6.21   Unison Tuning of the Guitar, **61**
6.22   Harmonic Tuning of the Guitar, **61**

Chapter 7   Wind Instruments   **67**

7.1   The Evolution of Woodwind Instruments, **67**
7.2   Open and Closed Tube Resonance, **70**
7.3   Determining the Resonant Frequency, **71**
7.4   Types of Bores, **73**
7.5   The Sound Sources: Vibrating Reed or Reeds, an Edge Tone, or Buzzing Lips, **74**
7.6   Woodwind Instruments: Flute and Piccolo, Clarinet, Saxophone, Oboe, English Horn, Bassoon, **74**
7.7.   The Evolution of Brass Instruments, **79**
7.8   Brass Instruments: Trumpet, Cornet, French Horn, Trombone, Tuba, **82**

Chapter 8   The Pipe Organ   **91**

8.1   The Evolution of the Pipe Organ, **91**
8.2   Construction of the Pipe Organ, **91**
8.3   Operation of the Organ Console, **93**
8.4   Organ Pipes, **94**
8.5   Performing on the Organ, **95**
8.6   The Electric Organ, **95**

Chapter 9   The Voice   **97**

9.1   Forced Inhalation (Inspiration), **97**
9.2   Forced Exhalation (Expiration), **98**
9.3   Lung Capacities, **98**
9.4   Vocal Sound Production, **99**
9.5   Vocal Classifications, **100**

Chapter 10   Percussion Instruments   **105**

10.1   The Evolution of Percussion Instruments, **105**
10.2   Membranophones, **109**
10.3   Membranophones of Definite Pitch, **111**
10.4   Membranophones of Indefinite Pitch, **111**
10.5   Idiophones of Definite Pitch: Tuning Fork, Orchestra Bells, Xylophone, Marimba, Bell Lyra, Vibraphone, Celesta, and Chimes, **112**
10.6   Idiophones of Indefinite Pitch: Cymbals, Triangle, Tambourine, Traps, **115**
10.7   Evolution of Bells, **116**

Chapter 11   Electronic Music   **125**
    11.1   Sound Sources, **125**
    11.2   Sound Modifiers, **126**
    11.3   Time Modifiers, **126**

Chapter 12   The Hearing Process   **127**
    12.1   The Structure of the Hearing Process, **127**
    12.2   The Dynamics of Hearing, **128**
    12.3   Subjective or Aural Harmonics, **129**
    12.4   Measurement of Hearing: The Audiogram, **129**
    12.5   Decibels, **130**
    12.6   The Phon, **131**
    12.7   Binaural and Stereophonic Sound, **131**
    12.8   Masking, **132**
    12.9   Pitch and Frequency Discrimination, **133**
    12.10 Absolute and Relative Pitch, **133**

Chapter 13   The Vibrato: Musical Ornamentation   **137**

Chapter 14   Recording   **139**
    14.1   Disc Recording, **139**
    14.2   Tape Recording, **139**
    14.3   Sound on Film, **142**
    14.4   Microphone and Speaker Placement for Stereo, **143**

Chapter 15   Architectural Acoustics   **147**
    15.1   Site Survey, **147**
    15.2   Sound Isolation: Airborne Sounds, **149**
    15.3   Solidborne Sound, **151**
    15.4   Sound Reflection within a Room, **152**
    15.5   Reverberation, **152**
    15.6   A Hypothetical Problem, **152**
    15.7   Miscellaneous Factors to Consider, **156**

Chapter 16   Sound Pollution   **163**

Appendixes   **167**
    Table of Sines, **167**
    Graph Relating Temperatures Fahrenheit and Centigrade (Celsius), **168**
    Pipe Length versus Fundamental Frequency in Hz., **169**
    Formulas for the Square, Triangular and Sawtooth Waves, **170**
    Table of Logarithms, **170**

Glossary   **175**

Preface

Initially the course "Acoustics of Music," for which this book was written, was intended to provide the music student with an understanding of musical sounds, their production, transmission and reception. However, with the course being offered in the General Education program, class enrollments increased (presently 300 per semester), the majority being from outside the School of Music. This required an assumption that the students knew little, if anything, about music; any musical concepts would have to be taught in the class. Also, with enrollments from every department in the university, many of which had their own association with sound, the scope of the course was expanded to recognize these areas and accommodating the students' interests, providing some discussions of non-musical areas as they related to acoustics.

The music student normally is not skilled, nor interested, in mathematics and physics; the non-music student knows little or nothing about the intricacies and technical vocabulary of the musician. Therefore, every effort has been made to present the material in a manner that can be understood by all. No special training in music or mathematics is required. In some instances, technical material is presented for those with the interest and background to understand, some relegated to the Appendix, but such material is not essential to understanding the material in this book. Where a technical understanding is necessary to grasp the material, it is explained.

It became evident that music students wanted to consider more deeply certain aspects of their special interests; those majoring in interior design or architecture wanted more study of architectural acoustics and building materials; those specializing in speech or audiology were primarily interested in those areas, and so on with those majoring in other departments. To provide an opportunity for each student to study any phase of acoustics in which he had great interest or need, a term paper or project was instituted which was optional, but earned the student extra credit. The student response to this opportunity was interesting and gratifying, so the optional term project was retained. Some of the best projects were presented to the entire class at the end of the term and were well received by the students.

After examining the available textbooks on this subject, it became evident that none dealt with the material considered significant for these students. Some books omitted essential material and some covered so much, and in such depth, that it would be inappropriate for a General Education course. This book evolved over a period of eight years with frequent revisions when found desirable, until it arrived at its present form.

The author hopes that this book will provide students with an understanding of the principles underlying the acoustics of music and related fields, and will stimulate them to question why things happen as they do, and promote a curiosity to investigate the unknown.

Acknowledgments

Due to the many areas of specialization, the author relied heavily on the expertise of a great many colleagues and friends without whose assistance this book could not have been written. It is essential and appropriate that they be named, along with their contributions, in heartfelt recognition for their friendly and generous assistance:

Marianne Bateman (Organ); Frank Bliven and Kent Gordon (Acoustic and Electric Guitar); John Boe (History); Will G. Bottje (Electronic Music); Dean Brown (Piano); Michael Hanes (Percussion); the late Lawrence Intravaia and George Hussey (Double Reeds); Frank Mainous and Robert Ottman (General suggestions and criticisms); Chau Yuan Li, Robert Mueller and Kent Werner (Scales and Intervals); Phillip Olsson and Melvin Siener (Brass). Not to be overlooked are the many other persons who contributed in some manner to the development of this book.

David Apple, Daryl Littlefield and Mark White (Photographs); Colleen Rayburn (Artist's sketches); and to the numerous institutions for photographs of instruments, each identified with the illustration.

Special thanks go to Arthur Lean, a friend and neighbor with several books to his credit, who read the entire manuscript with great care, offering suggestions and corrections.

For having provided me with laboratories to explore some of the phenomena heretofore unanswered, I am forever indebted to the late Joseph E. Maddy, President and Founder of the National Music Camp, Interlochen, Michigan; to the late John Guy Fowlkes, former Dean of the School of Education, University of Wisconsin-Madison.

Very special appreciation is given to my parents, the late Edgar B. Gordon, School of Music, University of Wisconsin-Madison, and the late Edna S. Gordon, who encouraged me from my youth to investigate, experiment and find the answers for myself.

Last, and most important of all, thanks go to my wife Janet, who has provided advice and encouragement, prodding when necessary, to help complete the manuscript.

Those who wonder,
And have the courage to pursue their thoughts,
Will unlock the mysteries of the unknown
And reveal the truth for all to come.

CHAPTER **1**

The Nature of Sound

1.1 Definition of Sound

Philosophers have long contemplated the answer to the question, "If a tree falls in the middle of a forest, does it make a sound?" The answer, of course, depends on the definition of sound. If sound is merely an acoustical disturbance, then the tree did make a sound. If it requires that someone hears the acoustical disturbance, then it did not make a sound. We shall adopt the latter definition.

Sound is that which is heard. It is the sensation produced by the stimulation of the organs of hearing by vibrations transmitted through the air or other media. As will be seen in a later chapter, actual hearing does not take place in the ear, but rather in the brain. The ear is merely a device which changes the variations in air pressure into electrical stimuli which, when received by the brain, produce the sensations of sound—hearing.

1.2 Perceptible Frequency Range

A young human, with a normal hearing mechanism, is sensitive to vibrations occurring at frequency rates between 20 and 20,000 vibrations per second (Hertz).* As one becomes older the highest frequency heard decreases, but the lowest heard remains virtually unchanged. There is some evidence to support the belief that at least some of the cause for loss of hearing at high frequencies is due to the increase of intense sounds in our present-day society. Much of the animal kingdom can hear sounds of frequency greater than we can. The dog can be taught to respond to a whistle which is ultrasonic for human beings; the nearly blind bat uses sonar by emitting short bursts of ultrasonic sounds which reflected by insects, locate their food, to be caught in flight as well as to avoid collisions with other objects.

1.3 Musical Sounds and Noise

If vibrations occur at a regular rate, as is produced by a plucked violin or guitar string, the sound heard has an identifiable pitch (the highness or lowness of a tone) and is defined as a musical sound. Most musical instruments, even the percussion instruments, produce mainly tone or musical sounds. A few produce noise.

Noise may be defined as the auditory sensation produced when the variations in air pressure occur at a rapid, random rate, such as rubbing two pieces of sandpaper together. The resulting

*"Hertz" is a unit of frequency, equal to one cycle per second, named after the German physicist, Heinrich Rudolph Hertz, 1857–94.

1

sound, noise, has no identifiable pitch. Some examples of noise are the sounds made when writing on, or erasing the blackboard, scraping feet on the floor, the speech sounds "ss," "sh," "k," "t," "p" and even in combinations with tone as in the sound "zz." "See the cow covered with a sheet" would sound like ""ee the ow overed with a ee" if noise were removed. Therefore, noise is essential in speech communication. Sometimes, noise is described as "pink" or "white" depending on the predominance of low or high frequencies.

1.4 Propagation or Transmission of Sound

If the end of a yardstick were held tightly over the edge of a table, then plucked so that it would vibrate with an up-and-down motion, on the upward swing the air molecules on the upper side would bunch together, causing a positive pressure. This pressure would be relieved through the air by one air molecule bumping into another, and that bumping into another, much as dominoes standing on end in a row, transfer their energy as they tip one another over. On the downward swing of the stick a negative pressure (partial vacuum) would be developed above this stick so the reverse action would take place. No molecule moves very far, but the energy transfer propagates with the velocity of sound, approximately one-fifth of a mile a second. It is fortunate, indeed, that the molecules of air themselves do not propagate with the speed of sound; otherwise a conversation would create quite a respectable wind which indeed sometimes seems to be the case. Of course, there is no transmission of sound in a vacuum, such as on the moon, since there are no gas molecules to transmit the energy.

1.5 The Sine Wave

If a pencil were attached to the vibrating end of the yardstick just described, and allowed to mark on a piece of paper being drawn horizontally at a uniform rate, the graph would represent the air pressure above the stick. If the motion of the stick did not die out, this regular up-and-down motion would draw a sine wave which represents a single frequency and is known as a pure tone. This pure tone has a hollow quality lacking in vitality, such as that of a whistle, flute, or a bottle being blown across its opening.

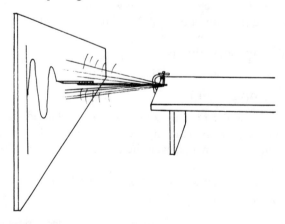

Figure 1.1. Vibrating yardstick tracing sine wave (Artist: Colleen Rayburn)

The sine wave represents a very fundamental type of variation or change, examples of which can be found in abundance: the movement of a pendulum or child's swing, the tide, bird's wing tips, fish tail, swaying of a tree, motion of a body walking.

1.6 Simple Graphic Construction of the Sine Wave[*]

The sine wave can be constructed graphically by drawing a circle, then projecting horizontal, parallel lines from the circumference at selected angles on to rectangular graph paper. Connecting the points of intersection will describe the sine wave. An examination of Fig. 1.2 will clarify the procedure.

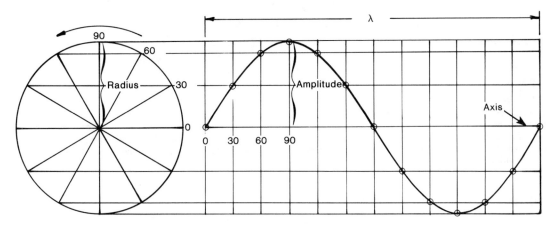

Figure 1.2.   Simple graphic construction of the sine wave

Note that the radius of the circle determines the maximum ordinate (the verticle distance from the axis) or displacement of the yard stick or vibrating body. This maximum ordinate is called the amplitude and represents the intensity of the tone. The distance between any point on a wave and the corresponding point on the next cycle is called the wavelength, represented by the Greek letter Lambda, λ. The wavelength is determined by the frequency of vibration. The third dimension is the shape of the wave which in this case is the sine wave. The mathematician would construct a sine wave using trigonometric tables.

1.7 The Audio Oscillator

In the laboratory, the instrument used to produce a sine wave is called an oscillator. The oscillator is an electrical device which produces a voltage that increases and decreases in amplitude at a regular rate. Some produce a sine wave variation in voltage and are heard as pure tones; others produce sawtooth, triangular, square waves and other variations. These latter types will be discussed further in the section dealing with electronic music. The most useful oscillator in the acoustics laboratory is the variable frequency audio oscillator which produces a sine wave (pure

[*]A Table of Sines may be found in the Appendix.

tone) of any frequency within the hearing range and with a wide control of amplitude (intensity). If your instructor has access to an audio oscillator, perhaps he will let you hear it varying in frequency from near zero Hertz up to an ultra sonic frequency (greater than 20,000 Hertz), just above the audible frequency range.

1.8 Physical and Psychological Parameters of Tone

The parameters mentioned above are terms describing the physical characteristics of sound; the psychological equivalent to these (what we perceive) are related as follows:

Table 1-A
Tonal Parameters

Physical	Psychological
Amplitude determines intensity	Loudness
Frequency determines wavelength	Pitch
Harmonic content* determines waveshape	Quality or Timbre

*When a number of pure tones of different but related frequencies (harmonics) sound together, the resulting disturbance in the air is no longer a pure tone of sine wave shape, but rather a complex wave representing a tone of altered quality.

1.9 The Velocity of Sound

Table 1-B
Velocity of Sound in Various Media

Material	$T°C$	Velocity feet/sec.	Material	$T°C$	Velocity feet/sec.
Copper	20	11670	Pine wood	—	10900
Iron	20	16820	Fir	—	15220
Soft gold	20	5717	Cork	—	1640
Silver	20	8553	Water	15	4714
Lead	20	4026	Air	20	1129
Brick	—	11980	Hydrogen	0	4165

In your study it may require that you convert temperature from Fahrenheit to Centigrade, or Centigrade to Fahrenheit. Following are the conversion formulae.

$$T°C = \frac{5}{9}(T°F - 32) \quad \text{or} \quad T°F = \frac{9}{5}T°C + 32$$

In the Appendix, a graph relating temperatures Fahrenheit and Centigrade (Celsius) is presented for your convenience.

1.10 Velocity of Sound in Air

The velocity of sound in air is little affected by changes in atmospheric pressure. There is only a slight increase in velocity with an increase in humidity as well as with an increase in intensity. However, the principal determiner of velocity is temperature so the other factors may be neglected for all practical purposes. The velocity of sound in air can be determined from the relationship $V = 1054 + 1.1\ T^\circ_F$ where V = velocity in feet/second, T = degrees Fahrenheit.

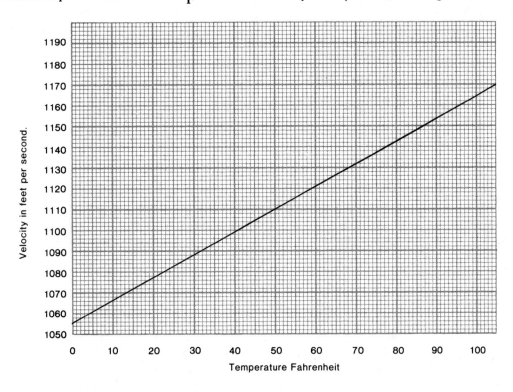

Figure 1.3.   Velocity of sound in air

1.11 Reflection of Sound from a Plane Surface

When a sound wave encounters a change in the medium through which it is traveling, it will be reflected. A wall presents a definite change in medium, from air to wood or plaster, and will be reflected very efficiently. When the sound is approaching the reflecting surface it is called an incident wave; after impact it is called a reflected wave. Fig. 1.4 illustrates sound impinging perpendicular to the reflecting surface, and at 45°. Note the angles of incidence "i" and reflection "r" made between the direction of propagation and the perpendicular to the surface.

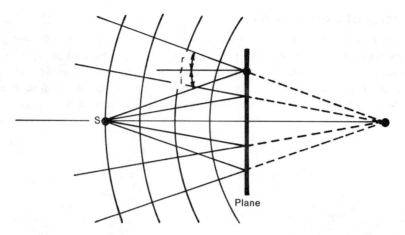

Figure 1.4. Refraction of sound from plane surface showing angles of incidence and reflection

A special instance of reflected sound is called an echo. If the distance a sound travels before reflection is great enough, a sound impinging on a large flat surface such as a building or rocky surface of a mountain, will return to the sound source with sufficient delay to be heard as an echo. It is an intelligible reflection of sound. When a person shouts "hello," the sound propagates to a flat surface some distance away and is reflected back to the sound source. This reflected sound is nearly the same as the original.

As an example, if we may assume a temperature of 42°F so the sound is traveling 1100 feet/second, and the echo is heard four seconds after the initial sound, then it must have taken two seconds to arrive at the reflecting surface and another two seconds for the return. In two seconds the sound would have traveled 2 × 1100 feet, or 2200 feet. Echo becomes apparent to the listener when the delay is about 0.1 seconds. In that time the sound would have traveled 110 feet so the surface would be 55 feet away. Therefore, as will be seen later in the section dealing with architectural acoustics, echo becomes a problem and must be dealt with if the distance to the reflecting surface is greater than 50 to 55 feet. Naturally, since temperature is the principal determiner of sound velocity, and the temperatures over the path of the sound are seldom constant, any calculations will be approximations.

1.12 Reflection from the Parabola and Ellipse

In addition to the plane surface, there are many other types of reflecting surfaces encountered in acoustical problems, two of which warrant special mention. These are the parabola and the ellipse. Both focus the sound.

The parabola, Fig. 1.5, is the shape employed in a spotlight reflector. If the light source is at the focal point, the rays will be reflected from the surface as parallel beams of light as in the spotlight. If the sound source is located at the focal point, the concentration of sound will be reflected as a beam making it quite directional. Note the angles of incidence and reflection made between the direction of propagation and the perpendicular to the tangent of the curve.

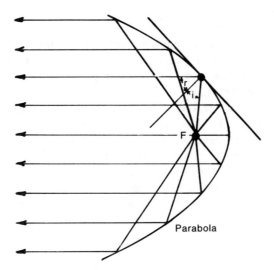

Figure 1.5. Reflection of sound from parabolic surface, showing angles of incidence and reflection

The parabolic reflector can serve as a collector of sound, like the "Big Ear" used on the football field. Sound from some distance away can be collected by the parabolic bowl which concentrates the sound at the focal point.

The ellipse, Fig. 1.6, has two foci. Energy originating at one focal point will be reflected at any point on the elliptical surface to the other focal point.

A more detailed discussion of the parabola and ellipse will be found in the Appendix.

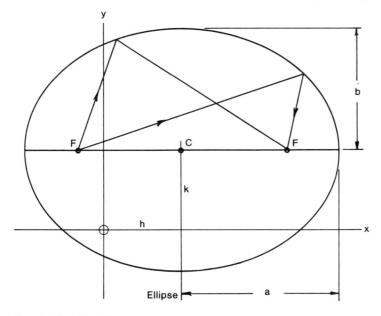

$$\frac{(x - h)^2}{a^2} + \frac{(y - k)^2}{b^2} = 1$$

Distance from center to either focus, $CF = a^2 - b^2$

Figure 1.6. The ellipse

1.13 Refraction of Sound

You may have noticed that sounds made by people in a canoe are heard loud and clear on shore. (Lovers beware!) Or, a political speech made on a hot, paved parking lot cannot be heard by the audience in the back of the crowd. This is due principally to refraction, the bending of sound due to differences in temperature.

In the case of the canoe on water, the air near the water is probably cooler than ten to twenty feet above the water. Since sound travels with a greater velocity in warm air than in cold, the sound is bent down towards the earth's surface. Examine Fig. 1.7. Imagine a two-wheel cart moving in the same direction as the sound. If the wheel further from the ground (warmer air) were to turn more rapidly, the cart would make an arc and be bent down towards the earth. If the air near the surface of the earth is warmer, such as above a paved parking lot in the sun, the cart's wheel nearest the earth would turn faster and aim upward. Thus, the speaker's voice is lost to his audience.

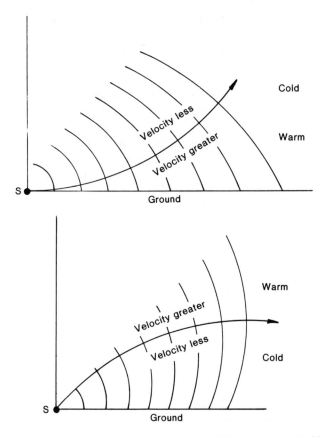

Figure 1.7.   Refraction of sound due to different sound velocities at different temperatures

1.14 Diffraction of Sound

Sound can be heard around a corner. The propagation of sound around a corner is called diffraction and is explained by Huygens* principle which states that every point on any wave front may be regarded as a source of the sound. See point "S" in Fig. 1.8. This explains how one can hear in back of a solid object. Understanding this phenomenon is important for future acoustical concepts, especially in architectural acoustics.

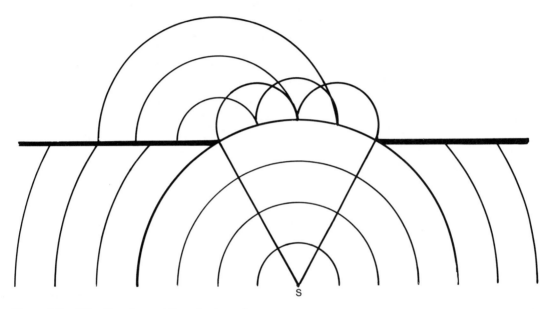

S

Figure 1.8. Diffraction of sound through an aperture

1.15 Doppler Effect

Christian Johann Doppler, 1803–1853, first espoused a theory explaining the different colors of the stars, as being dependent on their motion relative to the earth. Surely everyone has noticed the change in pitch due to the motion of the sound source, or the listener, or both. An observer standing beside the highway will hear a drop in the pitch of an automobile as it passes; the pitch of the signal bell at a railway crossing drops as the passenger passes. This is known as the Doppler effect.

Suppose that a 500 Hz tone is issuing from a loud speaker on top of an automobile. When the automobile and an observer are stationary, he will receive 500 impulses of sound per second. If the observer moves towards the stationary loud speaker, he will receive 500 impulses per second plus an additional number because of his motion. (Figure 1.9) This will produce a tone with a higher pitch than the sound source. If he moves away from the loud speaker he will intercept

*Christiaan Huygens (1629–1695), was a famous Dutch physicist and astronomer. He developed the wave theory of light from which came the "Principle of Huygens." Among his other accomplishments are the introduction of the pendulum to regulate clocks and the invention of the spiral watch-spring. His theorems on centrifugal force helped Newton formulate his law of gravitation.

fewer than 500 impulses per second, causing a lowering in pitch. Carried to the extreme, if he is moving away from the speaker with the speed of sound, he will receive no impulses at all.

Now consider the instance where the observer is stationary and the loud speaker moves towards him. Because of the motion of the loud speaker, the compressions are squeezed together shortening the wavelength, causing a rise in pitch. Note the relationship between frequency, wavelength and sound velocity.

$$f = \frac{v}{\lambda}$$ where f = frequency in cycles per second (Hz)
  v = velocity of sound in feet per second
  λ = wavelength in feet

If both the sound source and the observer are moving, and perhaps the wind is blowing, the net effect will be due to a combination of all three.

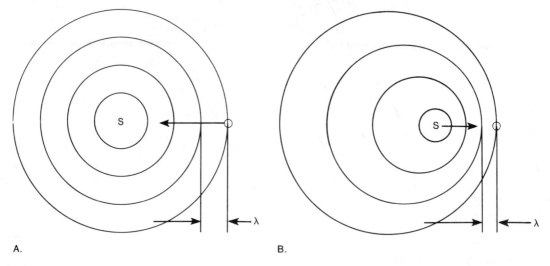

A.   B.

Figure 1.9.   Doppler effect. "A" is when observer is moving; "B" is when the sound source is moving.

Consider the example where an automobile, traveling 60 m/h, passes a stationary observer on the highway, and the engine is producing a sound of 500 Hz. The observer will hear a sound whose pitch is higher than the sound source because the sound waves are crowded together, shortening the wavelength. Let us determine the difference in frequency due to the motion of the sound source.

$$F = f_s \left(\frac{V \pm v_o}{V \pm v_s} \right)$$ where F is the observed frequency (Hz)
  f_s is the frequency of the sound source
  V is the velocity of sound in ft./sec.
  v_o is the velocity of the observer in ft./sec.
  v_s is the velocity of the sound source in ft./sec.

As the automobile approaches the observer, the pitch is higher than the sound source.

$$F = 500 \left(\frac{1100 - 0}{1100 - 88} \right) = 543.48 \text{ Hz}$$

After the automobile passes, the pitch drops.

$$F = 500 \left(\frac{1100 + 0}{1100 + 88} \right) = 462.96 \text{ Hz.}$$

This is a tone nearly a minor third lower in pitch.

Review Questions for Chapter 1. The Nature of Sound.

1. What is sound?

2. Over what range of frequencies can the normal young person hear?

3. What is meant by ultra-sonic and sub-sonic?

4. How is "noise" defined?

5. Identify the speech sounds which are noise. What about the sound "zzzz"? Why do some people omit the noise elements from their speech?

6. How is sound transmitted through the air?

7. Is sound transmitted in a vacuum? Why or why not?

8. What is the principal determiner of the velocity of sound in air?

9. How can one calculate the velocity of sound in air?

10. Does sound in copper or iron have a greater or lesser velocity than in air?

11. What is the "Doppler Effect"? Explain how it works. Describe the pitch heard with a relative motion between the sound source and/or the listener.

12. Define "echo."

13. Describe sound reflection from a parabolic reflector, or from an ellipse, when the sound originates at the focal points. How many focal points does a parabola have? How many focal points does an ellipse have?

14. Define refraction of sound. Why does this happen? When might sound be refracted?

15. Define diffraction of sound. What does Huygen's principle state? In what practical situation might the diffraction of sound be noticed?

16. What is a sine wave? How many frequencies does a sine wave represent? Describe two ways a sine wave could be graphed accurately. Name a motion in nature which follows a "sine wave."

17. What are the dimensions of a sine wave? What does each dimension represent in a musical tone? What does the Greek letter Lambda (λ) represent? What are the psychological equivalents to the physical parameters just named?

CHAPTER 2

The Harmonic, Partial, Overtone and Inharmonic

2.1 Definition of Harmonic, Partial, Overtone and Inharmonic

This chapter presents material that is probably the most important, the most basic, of any section in the book. It deals with what is known as the Harmonic Series.

Each of the terms—harmonic, partial, overtone and inharmonic—represents pure tones of sine wave or sinusoidal shape. Each tone has a pitch; they all have the same quality; they differ only in how their frequencies are related.

If we have a number of tone generators or electrical oscillators, each capable of producing a pure tone of any frequency in the audible range, they could be adjusted so as to produce a series of pure tones whose frequencies are 100, 200, 300, 400, . . . Hz. The frequencies are whole number multiples of the lowest frequency.

Employing the term "partial," the 100 Hz tone is called the first partial, 200 Hz the second partial, and so on. (See Table 2-A.)

Employing the term "harmonic," the lowest frequency, 100 Hz, is called the fundamental, 200 Hz is the first harmonic, 300 Hz is the second harmonic, and so on. The justification for this becomes apparent in a later section when we discuss the playing of harmonics on a stringed instrument. The term is used loosely in many physics textbooks employing "harmonic" and "partial" interchangeably.

Any tone whose frequency exceeds that of the lowest, in other words is over the frequency of the lowest tone, is called an overtone. In other words, in the series of tones cited above, 100 Hz would be the fundamental or first partial, 200 Hz, 300 Hz, . . . , would be overtones or more accurately harmonic overtones. It is not necessary, however, that the frequencies of overtones be whole number multiples of the lowest frequency. As an example, a tone in the above series whose frequency is 337 Hz would not be a partial nor a harmonic, but it would be an overtone—an inharmonic overtone since the term inharmonic means "not harmonic." Therefore, any tone whose frequency is not a whole number multiple of the lowest frequency is called an inharmonic overtone. If the term "partial" is employed, the tonal series would be known as the partial series; if the term "harmonic" is employed, it would be known as the harmonic series; the generic term representing any of the series—harmonic or inharmonic—could be called the overtone series.

2.2 Pitches of the Tones of the Partial or Harmonic Series

If ten oscillators, tuned to the first ten tones of the partial series, are sounded one after another, they will produce pitches which are members of our musical scale. The musician has a series of nonsense names for the tones of the scale, syllables, which we will use to identify the

Table 2-A
The Partial and Harmonic Series

Partial	Harmonic	Frequency	Syllable	Interval
18	17	1188	Re	
17	16	1122		Major 2nd
16	15	1056	Do	
15	14	990	Ti	
14	13	924		Perfect 4th
13	12	858		
12	11	792	Sol	
11	10	726		Minor 3d
10	9	660	Mi	
9	8	594	Re	Major 2nd
8	7	528	Do	Major 2nd
7	6	462	(Flat)	Perfect 4th
6	5	396	Sol	
5	4	330	Mi	Minor 3d
4	3	264	Do	Major 3d
3	2	198	Sol	Perfect 4th
2	1	132	Do	Perfect 5th
1	Fundamental	66	Do	Octave

pitch of each partial. Each note of the ascending major scale is given a syllable name: Do, Re, Mi, Fa, Sol, La, Ti and Do. The last, being eight tones higher than the first, is one octave higher than the first. "Octave" means eight and refers to the eighth tone of what we call our diatonic scale.

To assist the singer, Guido d'Arezzo (c. 990 A.D.) used the initial syllables of the first six musical phrases of a well-known hymn to St. John the Baptist:

Ut queant laxis	Ut
resonare fibris	Re
Mira gestorum	Mi
famuli tuorum,	Fa
Solve polluti	Sol
labii reatum,	La
Sancte Joannes.	

English translation: That thy servants may freely sing forth the wonders of thy deeds, remove all stain of guilt from their unclean lips, O Saint John.

Each of these musical phrases began one step higher in pitch than the phrase before, and the first phrase began on the note we call "C." Ut was later changed to Do (except in France). The syllable Si was later assigned to the seventh tone of the scale and then was later changed to Ti.

Review Questions for Chapter 2. The Harmonic, Partial, Overtone and Inharmonic.

1. Describe "harmonic," "partial," "overtone" and "inharmonic." How are they related? What are the waveshapes of each?

2. What are the musical pitches of the members of the partial series? (Do, Re, Mi, etc.)

3. If the frequency of any tone is doubled, how much is the pitch changed?

CHAPTER 3

Musical Scales

3.1 Musical Intervals

In order to talk about scales, first one must understand the meaning of "interval." It may be defined as the difference in pitch between two tones. The interval identification indicates the number of scale tones included within this interval. Referring to Fig. 3.1 the C-major scale results from playing in succession the tones C, D, E, F, G, A, B, and C. The interval from C to D is called a 2nd; C to E is called a 3d, and so on. The smallest change in pitch results from the playing of C and C#, which is called a semitone, with C to D being a whole tone, or two semitones.

Probably the easiest scale to describe is the chromatic scale. Starting with any note on the piano, every adjacent tone is played in succession, ascending or descending in pitch. In this case, the intervals are all semitones. The symbol # is called a sharp which means the pitch has been raised one semitone; the symbol b is called a flat, meaning that the pitch has been lowered one semitone. Referring to Fig. 3.2 a portion of the chromatic scale would be: C, C# (or D^b), D, D# (or E^b), E, F, . . .

A refinement in the interval names requires that 2nd, 3ds, 4ths, and so on be further identified as major, minor, augmented and diminished. An interval of a major 3d consists of 4 semitones, C to E; an interval of a minor 3d consists of 3 semitones, C to E^b.

Intervals of the 2d, 3d, 6th and 7th can be major, minor, augmented or diminished. Intervals of the 4th, 5th and octave can be perfect, augmented or diminished. Figure 3.1 should help to clarify the foregoing material.

3.2 Musical Scales

The major scale with which you are probably the most familiar is called the diatonic major scale. It consists of eight tones ascending or descending in order of pitch, and contains five whole tone, and two semitone intervals. These tones are represented by the syllables Do, Re, Mi, Fa, Sol, La, Ti, and Do. As an example, the scale of C-major uses all the white keys on the piano beginning with C and ascending to D, E, F, G, A, B, and C. There are many scales which can be played on the piano besides the scale of C-major. Following, in Figure 3.2, are some of the more usual. The scale pitches are the same ascending and descending with the exception of the melodic minor scale in which the 6th and 7th tones are raised when ascending in pitch, and lowered a semitone each when descending.

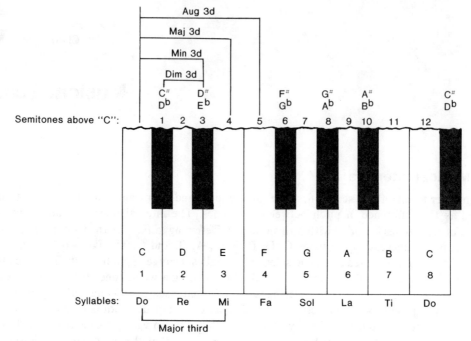

Figure 3.1 The piano keyboard

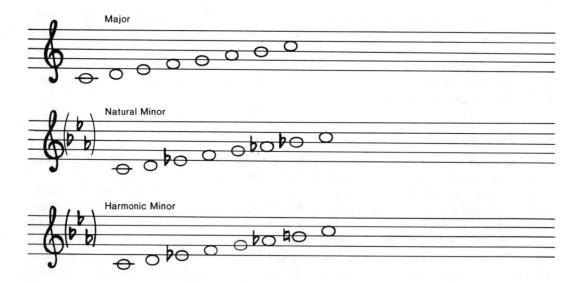

Figure 3.2. The principal scales

Figure 3.2—Continued

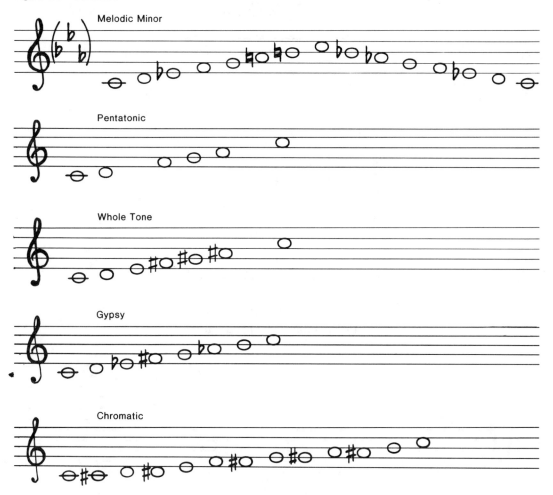

3.3 Pitch Octave Identification

When one refers to the pitch "C," not enough information is given to indicate which "C" on the piano keyboard we are referring to. A number of systems have been developed to identify the correct pitch.

In this book, the U.S.A. Standard system is employed. The lowest "C" on the piano has a frequency of 32.7 Hz (vibrations per second). One octave lower is 16.35 Hz, which is the lowest "C" that can be heard (or felt). That "C" is given the subscript of "0," (C_0), and all the tones contained in the octave above will carry the same subscript until the next "C" is reached. See Table 3-A.

Table 3-A
Pitch Subscript Notation

Hertz	*Subscript Notation*	
.	.	
.	.	
.	.	
130.81	C_3	
65.41	C_2	$\begin{cases} D_1 \\ C_1 \end{cases}$
32.70	C_1	$\begin{cases} B_0 \\ A_0 \end{cases}$
16.35	C_0	$\begin{cases} G_0 \\ F_0 \\ E_0 \\ D_0 \\ C_0 \end{cases}$

Table 3-B
Pitch Octave Identification

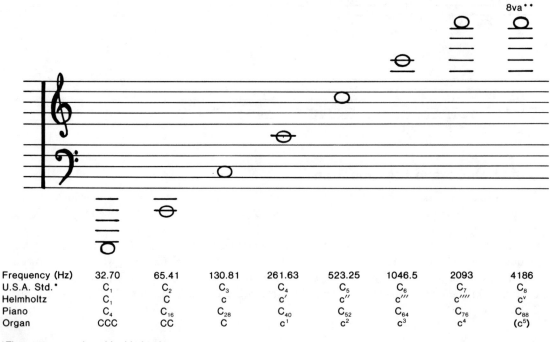

Frequency (Hz)	32.70	65.41	130.81	261.63	523.25	1046.5	2093	4186
U.S.A. Std.*	C_1	C_2	C_3	C_4	C_5	C_6	C_7	C_8
Helmholtz	C_1	C	c	c'	c''	c'''	c''''	c^V
Piano	C_4	C_{16}	C_{28}	C_{40}	C_{52}	C_{64}	C_{76}	C_{88}
Organ	CCC	CC	C	c^1	c^2	c^3	c^4	(c^5)

*The system employed in this book.
**8 va means "one octave higher"

3.4 Pythagorean Scale*

Phythagoras, the Greek philosopher-mathematician (c. 500 B.C.), believed that everything could be explained by numbers. He noted that a taut string, such as a violin string, if divided to vibrate in segments of equal length (as is the case when playing "harmonics"), produced pitches found pleasant and satisfying to the ear. A taut string, vibrating in one segment, will produce its fundamental pitch. If it vibrates in two segments, by touching the string lightly at its center, it sounds one octave higher than the fundamental—the pitch of the second partial; divided into three parts the pitch produced is one octave and a fifth higher than the fundamental—the pitch of the third partial; divided into four parts produced the pitch of the second octave. An octave is composed of a perfect fifth plus a perfect fourth. When intervals are added their frequency ratios are multiplied; thus a fifth plus a fourth (an octave) is $3/2 \times 4/3 = 12/6 = 2$. Note, from Table 2-A, the numbers of the partials provide the frequency ratios of the musical intervals.

Starting on C_4, the consecutive intervals of a fifth (seven semitones higher) are G, D, A, E, and so on until arriving at B#, which is the enharmonic equivalent of C, twelve intervals of a fifth higher. This is diagramed in Fig. 3.3. Interestingly, this higher "C_{11}," whose multiplying factor

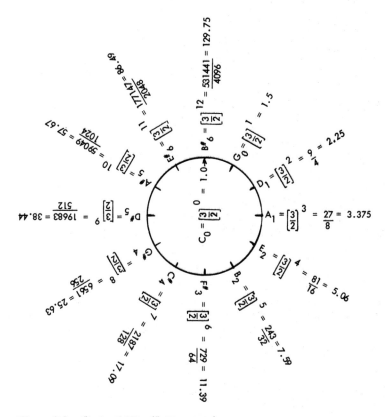

Figure 3.3.   Circle of fifths (Pythogorean)

*The Pythagorean Scale is presented for its historical interest.

is 129.7463 · · · is not a true octave, which would be 128.0. This discrepancy is called the Pythagorean Comma, which is

$$\frac{(3/2)^{12}}{2^7} = \frac{129.7463}{128} \cdots = 1.01364 \cdots$$

where 2^7 is the frequency of the 7th octave higher, and $(3/2)^{12}$ should produce the same pitch.

Similar results can be obtained by descending by fourths whose frequency ratio is $4/3 = 1.33 \cdots$

3.5 The Just Scale, or The Scale of Ptolemy, c. 130 A.D.

The 4th, 5th, 6th and 8th partials sound the pitches Do, Mi, Sol and Do respectively. This chord is known as the tonic chord (or major triad). From this we can obtain the frequency ratios for the musical intervals.

Partial Interval

Do	8	
		fourth (8/6) = 1.33 . . .
Sol	6	
		minor third (6/5) = 1.20
		fifth (6/4) = 1.5 octave (8/4) = 2.0
Mi	5	
		major third (5/4) = 1.25
Do	4	

The ratio of the partials producing any given musical interval will provide the correct frequencies of the tones involves. For instance, $\frac{\text{Sol}}{\text{Mi}} = \frac{6}{5}$ So if Mi = A_4 = 440 Hz, then the frequency of Sol, $C_5 = \frac{6}{5} \times 440 = 528$ Hz. It will probably be easier to use the factors $6/5 = 1.20$ for a minor 3d; $5/4 = 1.25$ for a major 3d; $6/4 = 1.5$ for a 5th; $2/1 = 2.0$ for the octave. If one multiplies the frequency by the factor, the frequency of the higher pitched tone is determined; if one divides the frequency by the factor; the frequency of the lower pitched tone is determined.

To calculate the frequencies for the C-major scale, begin with the F-major triad (F-A-C), which included the standard pitch, A = 440 Hz. The interval F-A is a major third (1.25); the interval A-C is a minor third (1.20) and the interval F-C is a perfect fifth (1.5). Employing these multiplying factors, the frequencies for F and C are obtained. To drop an octave in pitch, from C_5 to C_4, the frequency of C_5 is divided by 2.0. We can now calculate the frequencies for the C-major triad, C-E-G and the G-major triad G-B-D in the same manner. The frequency of D_5 is divided by 2.0 to obtain D_4. This completes the C-major scale.

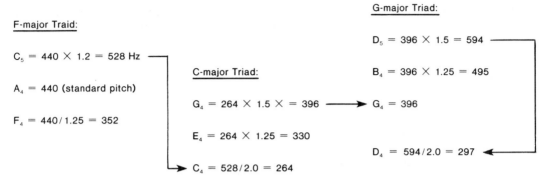

G-major Triad:

$D_5 = 396 \times 1.5 = 594$ ────┐

F-major Traid:

$C_5 = 440 \times 1.2 = 528$ Hz ──┐

C-major Triad:

$B_4 = 396 \times 1.25 = 495$

$A_4 = 440$ (standard pitch)

$G_4 = 264 \times 1.5 \times = 396$ ──→ $G_4 = 396$

$F_4 = 440/1.25 = 352$

$E_4 = 264 \times 1.25 = 330$

$D_4 = 594/2.0 = 297$ ←────

$C_4 = 528/2.0 = 264$

See Table 3-B for these frequencies arranged in an ascending scale.

Among the disadvantages of the Just scale are: (1) one perfect fifth, d–a, in the C-major scale is dissonant; (2) the C-major scale has two different whole tones; and (3) modulation to distantly related keys is not possible. Probably the only use made of Just intonation is by string players—particularly string quartets—because the beat tones produced are all members of the harmonic series and make for a smoothness in quality.

3.6 Tempered Scale

With the invention of the keyboard instrument, similar to the piano, where $C^\#$ and Db are enharmonic equivalents and are played with the same key and therefore must have the same pitch or frequency, it was necessary to develop a "compromise" scale which sounded as well in tune in one key as in another. An octave was divided into 12 equal semitones. Since pitch and frequency are related exponentially, this required merely extracting the 12th root of 2.0 (where 12 represents the number of semitones to the octave, and 2.0 is the ratio of frequency for an octave). The multiplier turns out to be 1.05946 . . . or roughly 1.06. Beginning with our standard pitch, A = 440 Hz, the frequency of a semitone higher will be $440 \times 1.06 = 466.4 = A^\#$ or Bb; 440/ $1.06 = 4.15.1 = $ Ab or $G^\#$; $466.4 \times 1.06 = 494.4 = $ B; $415.1/1.06 = 391.6 = $ G and so on. (See Table 3-D.) Note that with the exception of the octave, the tones of the tempered scale are not exactly in tune in any key, because of the "roughness" due to beats, but our ears seem to be able to tolerate the slight errors.

3.7 Cents

When working with intervals, calculations are simplified by expressing the intervals in terms of fractions of a semitone. To do this, the frequency ratios are converted to cents (¢) where by definition one tempered semitone equal 100¢.Since there are 12 semitones in an octave, there are 1200¢ to the octave

Referring to the drawing of a piano keyboard, one finds there are four semitones in a major third interval (C to E), which is 400¢; there are three semitones in a minor third interval (C to E^b), which is 300¢. Adding a major third and a minor third produces an interval of a fifth (C to G), which has seven semitones (700¢): 400¢ + 300¢ = 700¢.

Conversion of Just intervals to cents requires a simple calculation employing the following relationship, $\cent = 3986 \log f_2/f_1$. The ratio of frequencies for a major third $= 1.25$. Therefore, $\cent = 3986 \log 1.25$. From the log table in the Appendix, $\log 1.25 = 0.097$; $\cent = 3986 (.097) = 386+$. The same procedure may be employed with Pythagorean pitches.

Incidentally, note the difference between the Just and tempered major thirds, $400 - 386+ = 13+$. The tempered tone is higher in pitch.

Without converting to cents, it is possible to add two intervals by multiplying their frequency ratios. As an example, add a Just major third ($5/4 = 1.25$) to a Just minor third ($6/5 = 1.20$), which results in an interval of a fifth ($6/4 = 1.50$).

$$\frac{5}{4} \times \frac{6}{5} = \frac{6}{4} = 1.50 \text{ or } 1.25 \times 1.20 = 1.50$$

3.8 Other Tempered Scales

The whole-tone scale (C, D, E, F#, G#, Bb), the Scottish and Oriental pentatonic scales (C, D, F, G, A), and the Indian quarter-tone scale divide the octave in a different manner from the diatonic or chromatic scales. Even so, the whole-tone and pentatonic scales can be played on the piano keyboard.

It is not necessary for a scale to have 12 semitones to the octave. The frequencies of scale tones for any number of intervals to the octave are easily obtained. The same relationship is used as when deriving our equally-tempered scale, the multiplying factor being $\sqrt[n]{2.0}$ where "n" equals the number of intervals to the octave and 2 equals the frequency ratio of one octave. Table 3-D provides the tonal frequencies for various scales. An instrument may be tuned to these frequencies by adjusting an audio oscillator to the derived frequencies and tuning the instrument to the pitches produced.

3.9 Tendency Tones or Pitches

With a melodic instrument, such as the violin and most other orchestral instruments, where the frequency of the tones can be adjusted at will, we find performing artists employ pitches which deviate somewhat from the mathematically derived scales. Usually, because of the psychological "pull" upward, the 3rd and 7th tones of the scale are a little sharp when ascending in pitch, and a little flat when descending. Of course, when an instrument is performing with a keyboard instrument, which must employ tempered intonation, undoubtedly the performer employs tempered intonation or his instrument would sound out-of-tune with the piano.

If a pitch vibrato (a periodic variation in pitch occurring at a rate of approximately five or six per second) is employed by the violinist, the slight discrepancies in intonation are less noticeable, just as pitch inaccuracies are "covered up" by very rapid performance, where the duration of a tone lasts but a fraction of a second. See "The Vibrato: Musical Ornamentation."

3.10 Instruments Employing Tempered Intonation

Since the performer cannot adjust the pitch of factory-tuned instruments (piano, xylophone, chimes, pipe organ, harp), he must employ tempered intonation to permit changing (modulating) to other keys and still sound reasonably well in tune.

Table 3-C
Just, Pythagorean and Tempered Scales

Tone	Interval	Just		Pythagorean		E.T.*	Cents			Frequencies (Hz) Standard: A = 440 Hz		
		Multiplier: $f_2:f_1$	To calculate cents log $f_2:f_1$	Multiplier: $f_2:f_1$	To calculate cents log $f_2:f_1$	Multiplier $f_2:f_1$	Just	Pyth	E.T.	Just	Pyth	E.T.
C (do)	Perf oct	2:1=2.0	0.30103	2:1=2.0	0.30103	2.000	1200	1200	1200	528	521.48	523.25
C♭	Dim oct											
B♯	Aug 7th											
B(ti)	Maj 7th	15:8=1.875	0.27300	243:128=1.898	0.27840	1.888	1088.3	1109.8	1100	495	495	493.88
B♭	Min 7th	9:5=1.80	0.25527			1.782	1017.6		1000			466.16
A♯	Aug 6th											
A(la)	Maj 6th	5:3=1.66..	0.22185	27:16=1.6875	0.22724	1.682	884.4	905.9	900	440	440	440
A♭	Min 6th	8:5=1.60	0.20412			1.587	813.7		800			415.30
G♯	Aug 5th											
G(sol)	Perf 5th	3:2=1.50	0.17609	3:2=1.5	0.17609	1.498	702.0	702.0	700	396	391.11	392.00
G♭	Dim 5th											
F♯	Aug 4th	25:18=1.388	0.14267			1.414	568.7		600			369.99
F(fa)	Perf 4th	4:3=1.33..	0.12494	4:3=1.33..	0.12494	1.335	498.0	498.0	500	352	347.65	349.23
F♭	Dim 4th											
E♯	Aug 3rd											
E(mi)	Maj 3rd	5:4=1.25	0.09691	81:64=1.26563	0.10231	1.260	386.3	407.8	400	330	330	329.63
E♭	Min 3rd	6:5=1.20	0.07918			1.189	315.6		300	315.6		311.13
D♯	Aug 2nd											
D(re)	Maj 2nd	9:8=1.125	0.05115	9:8=1.125	0.05115	1.122	203.9	203.9	200	297	293.33	293.66
D♭	Min 2nd											
C♯	Semitone	25:24=1.0417	0.01773			1.059	70.67		100			277.18
C(do)	Unison	1:1=1.0	0.00000	1:1=1.0	0.00000	1.000	0.0	0.0	0	264	260.74	261.63

*$(12\sqrt{2})^n$ where n = number of semitone intervals above Do.

25

Table 3-D
Frequencies of Tones for Tempered Scales
Employing from One to Twelve Intervals to the Octave
Based on A = 440 Hz

$\sqrt[1]{2}=$	$\sqrt[2]{2}=$	$\sqrt[3]{2}=$	$\sqrt[4]{2}=$	$\sqrt[5]{2}=$	$\sqrt[6]{2}=$	$\sqrt[7]{2}=$	$\sqrt[8]{2}=$	$\sqrt[9]{2}=$	$\sqrt[10]{2}=$	$\sqrt[11]{2}=$	$\sqrt[12]{2}=$
2.000	1.414	1.2599	1.1892	1.1487	1.1225	1.1041	1.0905	1.0801	1.0718	1.0650	1.05946
880.000:A	880.000:A	880.000:A	880.000:A	880.000:A	880.000:A	880.000:A	880.000:A	880.000:A	880.000:A	880.000:A	880.000:A
440.000:A	622.254:D#	698.456:F	739.989:F#	766.084	783.991:G	797.037	806.964	814.770	821.069	826.259	830.609:G#
	440.000:A	554.365:C#	622.254:D#	666.915	698.456:F	721.895	739.989:F#	754.375	766.084	775.800	783.991:G
		440.000:A	523.251:C	580.583	622.254:D#	653.837	678.573	698.456:F	714.782	728.423	739.989:F#
			440.000:A	505.427	554.365:C#	592.196	622.254:D#	646.683	666.915	683.939	698.456:F
				440.000:A	493.883:B	536.366	570.609	598.748	622.254:D#	642.171	659.255:E
					440.000:A	485.799	523.251:C	554.365:C#	580.583	602.954	622.254:D#
					(Whole tone scale)	440.000:A	479.823	513.273	541.704	566.133	587.330:D
							440.000:A	475.226	505.427	531.559	554.365:C#
								440.000:A	471.580	499.098	523.251:C
									440.000:A	468.618	493.883:B
										440.000:A (Piano scale)	466.164:A#
											440.000:A

Further tempered multipliers

$13\sqrt{2} = 1.054766$
$14\sqrt{2} = 1.050757$
$15\sqrt{2} = 1.047294$
$16\sqrt{2} = 1.044274$
$17\sqrt{2} = 1.041616$
$18\sqrt{2} = 1.039259$
$19\sqrt{2} = 1.037155$
$20\sqrt{2} = 1.035265$
$21\sqrt{2} = 1.033558$
$22\sqrt{2} = 1.032008$
$23\sqrt{2} = 1.030596$
$24\sqrt{2} = 1.029302$

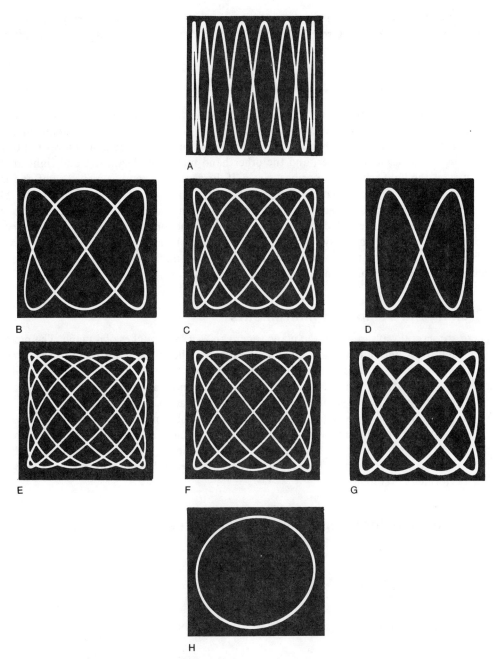

Figure 3.4. Lissajous figures. (A) Lissajous figure of two sine waves, frequency ratio 8:1; a three octave interval; (B) Lissajous figure of frequency ratio 3:2 (an interval of a perfect fifth); (C) Lissajous figure of frequency ratio 5:3 (an interval of a major sixth); (D) Lissajous figure of an octave, frequency ratio 2:1; (E) Lissajous figure of a minor third, frequency ratio 6:5; (F) Lissajous figure of a major third, frequency ratio 5:4; (G) Lissajous figure of frequency ratio 4:3 (an interval of a perfect fourth); (H) Lissajous figure of a unison, frequency ratio 1:1.

Later, it will be shown that brass instruments produce tones of the partial series, representing Just intonation. Adjustment requires the performer to "lip" the tone until it sounds acceptably in tune.

3.11 Tuning Just Intonation

The French physicist, Jules A. Lissajous (1822–1880), investigated the designs made by two sine waves, moving at right angles to one another, having a frequency ratio of small integers. Consider the design made by a flashlight beam, shining on the wall. If one hand moves the beam up and down in a sinusoidal manner, and the other hand moves the beam left and right at the same frequency, the light spot will describe a circle. If, however, the beam is moved right-and-left with twice the frequency it is moved up-and-down, the light spot will describe a figure-eight. The ratio of the number of loops across the top to the number on the side provides the ratio of the two frequencies. These designs are called Lissajous figures. Since the tones of Just intonation (intervals of the partial series) are related by whole numbers (integers), the Lissajous figure provides an admirable and exact method for directly measuring and adjusting Just intonation. See Figure 3.4 for examples of Lissajous figures and their frequency ratios.

3.12 Tuning the Tempered Instruments

There are several ways in which the piano tuner can "set" the pitches of a piano. The method employed exclusively until a few years ago employed beats. The initial adjustment was set to just intonation, which provided smooth, inaudible beat tones, then to raise or lower the pitch until the correct number of beats was heard. Once the tones within an octave were tuned, those of other octaves, above and below, were set with the tuned octave by adjusting to zero beats.

With the development of a stroboscopic device (the Stroboconn), it is now possible to tune the tempered pitches visually and very accurately. Piano tuners occasionally deviate from the mathematically derived frequencies (expanded octaves) for the higher pitches, and others adhere strictly to the tempered frequencies. There is no hard-and-fast rule that governs this, but it depends upon the performer's preference.

Review Questions for Chapter 3. Musical Scales

1. What is a musical interval?

2. What is a semitone? A whole tone?

3. What is a major third? A minor third?

4. What are the syllable names for the tones of a major scale

5. What is a diatonic scale?

6. Identify by name the principal scales. What are the characteristics of each?

7. Explain the subscript notation employed in this book to identify the musical pitches. What is the subscript notation for "middle C"?

8. How did Pythagoras arrive at the frequencies for the scale? Are these frequencies correct?

9. What name is given to the "in tune" scale? Why is a piano not tuned to this scale? To what scale is the piano tuned?

10. How can one determine the frequencies for the Just C-major scale, given A = 440 Hz?

11. What is meant by "cents"? How are they used?

12. What is the multiplying factor for our tempered piano scale? How was it obtained?

13. If A = 440 Hz, what would be the frequencies of a tempered semitone higher, and a tempered semitone lower?

14. Given the frequency of a tone, how would you determine the Just frequencies of tones a major third higher, a minor third higher, a perfect fifth higher, an octave higher?

15. What is meant by "tendency tones or pitches"?

16. What instruments employ tempered intonation? Just intonation?

17. Explain Lissajous figures. How may they be employed in tuning Just intonation?

18. Given several Lissajous figures, be able to identify the musical intervals they represent.

19. What instrument measures tempered intonation directly?

20. If you wanted to invent a new scale with "n" tones to the octave, describe how you would determine the multiplier.

Chapter 4

Tone Quality

4.1 Complex Waves

You have seen the waveshape of a single frequency, the sine wave. Now consider two pure tones with frequencies of 100 Hz and 200 Hz (frequency ratio of 2:1) sounding simultaneously. They would graph individually as the sine waves shown in Fig. 4.1. Note that the wavelength of tone #2 is half that of tone #1, indicating the frequency of #2, 200 Hz, is twice that of #1, 100 Hz.

Select vertical lines (ordinates) at any position along the axis. Add the heights of the two ordinates algebraically and plot the sum for each. Connect these points with a smooth, solid line which represents the complex wave. A loud speaker cone, or the ear drum, will move back-and-forth like this complex wave. In Fig. 4.1 the amplitude of wave #1 was chosen to be twice that of #2. In Fig. 4.2 the amplitude of wave #2 is twice that of #1.

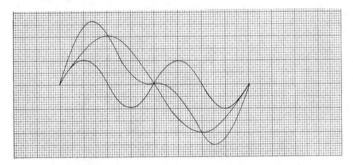

Figure 4.1. Addition of two pure tones, 100 and 200 Hertz (Amplitude ratio 2:1)

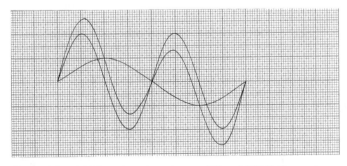

Figure 4.2. Addition of two pure tones, 100 and 200 Hertz (Amplitude ratio 1:2)

31

The shape of a sound wave indicates the partials sounding and their relative amplitudes. In other words, the waveshape is an exact, scientific picture of tone quality. It is possible to identify visually certain of the more intense partials of a complex wave and their approximate amplitudes. Examine the following waveshape, Fig. 4.3.

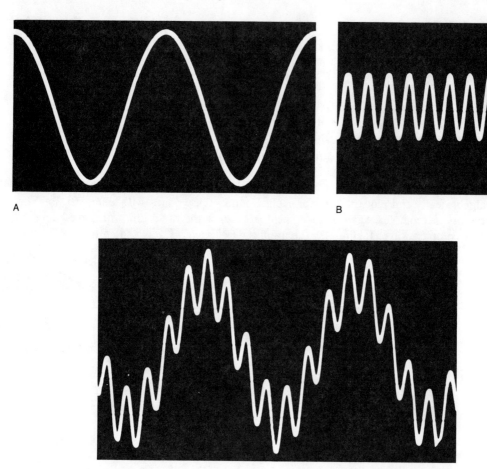

Figure 4.3. Synthesis of a complex wave. (A-B) A sine wave (pure tone); (C) Synthesis of the two sine waves, Figures A and B. Note frequency ratio is 7:1, a dissonant interval.

Complex waves may be observed on an oscilloscope (Fig. 4.5) permitting a rough visual analysis. To do this, count the "mountain peaks" per cycle in the following manner. The general shape of the wave in Fig. 4.4 is above the axis on the left, and below the axis on the right. This requires the presence of the first partial. Now, count the peaks per cycle of the next shorter wavelength. There are eleven per cycle, so the complex wave must be composed of the first and eleventh partials.

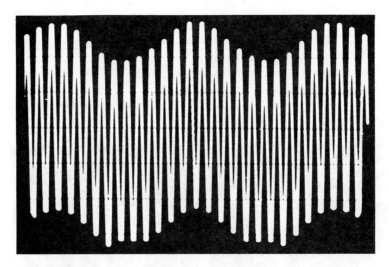

Figure 4.4.   Synthesis of two sine waves, frequency ratio 11:1. The amplitude of the higher frequency is much greater than the lower frequency.

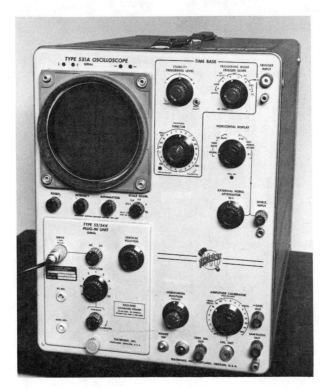

Figure 4.5.   An oscilloscope used for observing waveshapes (Photo by David Apple)

Eventually, with the addition of many partials, the complex wave can become so complicated it is difficult or impossible to make a visual analysis. Such analyses must be made mathematically or with the aid of mechanical or electronic harmonic analyzers.

The following waveshapes represent tones produced by several musical instruments. These are not the only waveshapes that a single instrument can produce, for the partial structure (quality) is a function of the pitch sounded, the intensity, the characteristics of the instrument, and the anatomy of the performer.

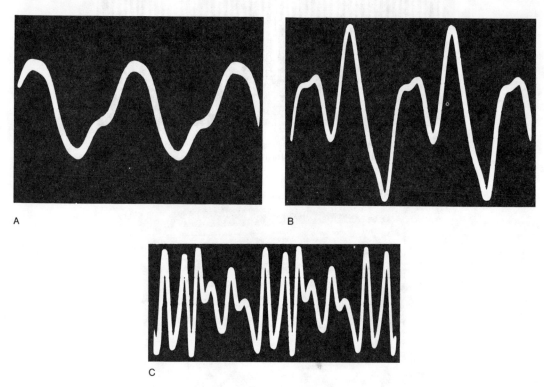

Figure 4.6.   (A) Oscillogram of a flute tone; (B) Oscillogram of a trumpet tone; (C) Oscillogram of an oboe tone

4.2 Phase

To introduce the concept of phase, consider as an example the wing tips of a bird moving up and down together—they are synchronized—they are in phase. Then, consider the ends of a teeter-totter moving in opposition—they are out-of-phase. Since one end of the teeter-totter starts moving up when the other end starts moving down, they are said to be completely out-of-phase, or 180° out-of-phase. Phase may be defined as a particular amount of advancement in a cycle, measured in degrees, and can vary from 0° to 360° depending upon their relative timing.

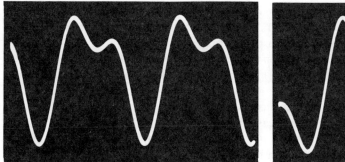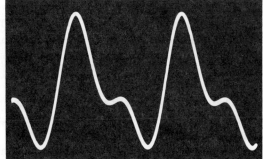

Figure 4.7. Oscillogram of a tone composed of the first and second partials, but with different phase relationships

4.3 Interference and Reinforcement

If two sine waves or tones of the same frequency are in phase, their ordinates add together so as to increase the amplitude (loudness) of the resulting tone. This would be maximum reinforcement. If the tones are out-of-phase to any degree, the resulting wave will have less amplitude than when in-phase, causing a reduction in loudness. When the waves are completely out-of-phase (180°), and have the same amplitudes, there will be a complete cancellation of sound, since the positive ordinates of one tone will be equal to the negative ordinates of the other tone. This occurs quite frequently, and when it does, complete silence results. This is complete interference.

4.4 Effect of Phase on Tone Quality

In an inspection of the waveshapes in Fig. 4.1A and B, in which the phase between the partials is different, it will be noted that the wave shape is dependent upon phase, even though the partials and their intensities are the same. The quality of a tone is dependent upon the partials sounding and their relative intensities—and not upon the phase relationships between the partials. Therefore, it might be possible to reproduce exactly a given tone aurally, even though perhaps not visually, due to differences in phase.

4.5 Resonance

An object, or air cavity, is said to be resonant if it is tuned to vibrate at certain frequencies which are known as the resonant frequencies. In other words, a pendulum is "tuned" to a frequency and is resonant whether it is swinging or not. A violin string will vibrate at a frequency to which it has been tuned, but does not have to be vibrating or making a sound to be resonant at this frequency. When it swings, it is resonating. A column of air such as that inside a test tube or pipe is resonant and by blowing across the open end, will produce a tone at its resonant frequency. If one blows harder, increasing the velocity of the air jet, the tone will jump to a higher pitch (a harmonic), so it is also resonant to this higher pitch.

Resonance, then, is a physical property of the body, the predisposition to vibrate at a particular frequency. Almost all bodies are resonant, even a bowl of jelly or a table top. Strike a wooden table top with the rubber eraser on the end of a pencil, then strike the seat of a chair. Note the difference in the pitches produced. The duration is so short it may be difficult or impossible to identify the pitch. However, if it is recorded at high speed, then played back at slow speed, the pitch will become identifiable.

There are many obvious examples of resonance about us. The swing in the park, the suspension bridge (soldiers break step when crossing it in case their footsteps are at the resonant frequency which would collapse the bridge), a bell or gong, guy wires steadying the TV antenna hum at their resonant frequencies, known as an Aeolian harp, are a few of the many examples.

4.6 Sympathetic Vibrations

If you push a child on a playground swing with your little finger at the frequency of the swing (or any sub multiple), with each impulse the amplitude of the swing will increase gradually until it reaches a maximum, depending upon the strength of the impulses you supply. In this example, the source of energy is supplied directly to the resonant body (the swing). If an intermediate substance, such as air, transfers the energy from the source to the resonant body, the resonant body will vibrate also. This is called sympathetic vibration. We have many examples about us such as the rattling of windows when a truck drives by, the vibration of a taut string due to the sounding of a tone whose frequency is the same as the resonant frequency of the taut string. The taut guy wires attached to the television antenna, or the telephone lines, occasionally will hum when the wind blows. If the child on the playground swing is given an impulse (push) every second vibration, or every third vibration, or any other sub multiple, the swing will begin to move with its natural resonant frequency. If a taut string is tuned to resonate at 500 Hz, then 500, 250, 125 . . . Hz will cause the taut string to vibrate at 500 Hz. If 1000 Hz is sounded which is a whole number multiple of the string's resonant frequency (500 Hz), the string will vibrate at 1000 Hz, the first harmonic of the string's fundamental frequency, but not at 500 Hz. At 500 Hz, the first impulse will start it moving in one direction, then the second impulse will be in opposition and will stop the vibration.

4.7 Formant Resonance

The theory of tone quality is based on the assumption that the relative intensities of the harmonics (harmonic spectrum) for any pitch remain constant or fixed. Actually, for most instruments this is not the case because they have fixed resonators which amplify certain bands of frequencies (formant regions) regardless of the frequency of the fundamental. Therefore, only the harmonics whose frequencies lie within these formants will be amplified. This means, of course, that each tone will have its unique quality—different from all other tones—due to formant resonance. Employing the harmonic theory of tone quality, all tones would have the same, pre-set quality like the Hammond Organ.

A careful study of Figures 4.8 and 4.9 will illustrate the differences between the harmonic and the formant theories of tone quality.

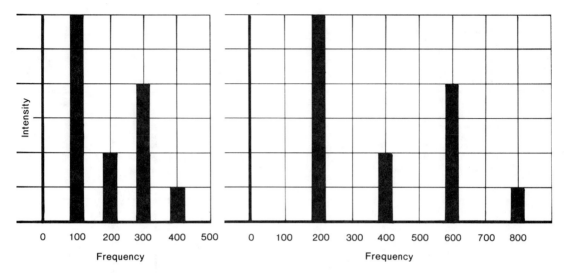

Figure 4.8. Two tonal spectra illustrating the harmonic theory of tone quality. (Note the identical distribution of energy.)

4.8 Aural Analysis of Complex Tones

If one were to sing a nasal tone, sustaining the sound "oh," then change the position of the lips, the oral cavity (mouth) can be tuned to resonate and amplify the individual partials. With a little practice you can demonstrate this yourself. It is sometimes difficult for the listener to hear the specific pitches as they are resonated because we are so in the habit of synthesizing complex sounds into the total quality of a vowel that it is difficult to hear the components individually. However, if you will listen, not to the pitch being sung, but rather to the higher pitches which form chords, these partials can be identified. It should be obvious that the difference between the various vowel sounds is merely a difference in the partials being sounded—in other words, in the tone quality.

4.9 Scientific Analysis of Tone Quality

An aural analysis of tone quality is highly subjective, recognizing as real, the subjective tones produced, and entirely inadequate for any accurate, scientific work. To effect an accurate analysis, one of the following methods may be employed: (1) a mathematical analysis, which is a very tedious process, and not recommended except for those trained in mathematics; (2) the use of the Henrici Analyzer, in essence the same procedure as the mathematical analysis, which traces the complex waveshape and breaks it into the various sine and cosine functions—also tedious; (3) an electronic analyzer with which the tone is scanned over the audio frequency range, and a band-pass filter makes possible an accurate indication of the amplitudes of the various partials. This third method is the fastest, easiest to use, and probably the most accurate.

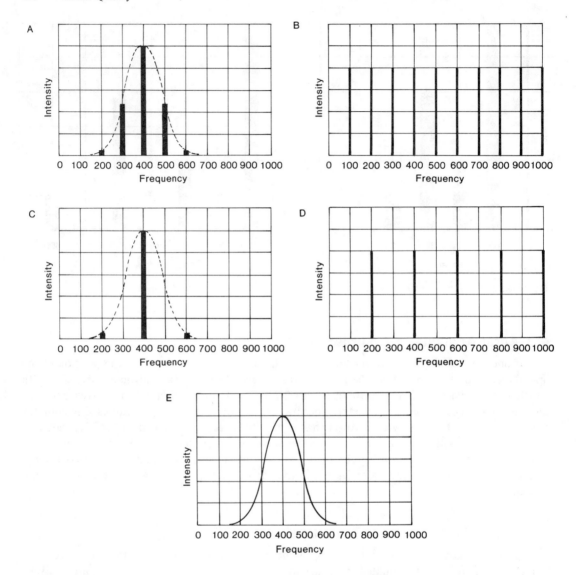

Figure 4.9. Tonal spectra illustrating formant resonance. (A) Intensity of partials heard (Fundamental = 100 Hz.); (B) Intensity of partials generated (Fundamental = 100 Hz.); (C) Intensity of partials heard (Fundamental = 200 Hz.); (D) Intensity of partials generated (Fundamental = 200 Hz.); (E) Response of the resonator.

4.10 Noise

As defined earlier, noise results not from regular, but from randomly occuring disturbances in the air. Rubbing two pieces of sandpaper together provides a good example of noise; in speech, the unvoiced consonants are noise; the hiss made by a violin bow when very high pitched tones

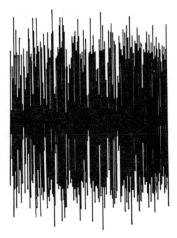

Figure 4.10. Noise, as seen on
the oscilloscope

are being played is noise; the rattle made by the snares on a snare drum and the breathy quality of a vocal tone are noise. Many sounds which are loosely referred to as noise are strictly speaking, not truly noise.

Noise can be detected on the oscilloscope as "grass." It shows as a blurred, fuzzy, moving line which is apparent on a waveshape at the peak, the trough, or wherever the wave tends to flatten horizontally. It is interesting to note that noise can be seen on the oscilloscope even when it can not be heard by the ear. For this reason, the oscilloscope serves as an excellent diagnostic tool in tonal analysis.

Review Questions for Chapter 4. Tone Quality

1. Name some instruments that produce a pure tone.

2. What are the physical determiners of tone quality?

3. Is it possible to obtain a scientifically accurate picture of tone quality? How?

4. What is meant by "synthesis?" By "analysis?"

5. Is it possible to effect a visual analysis of a complex wave? Under what conditions?

6. What electronic instrument provides a picture of tone quality?

7. What is meant by "phase?" Does the phase between partials alter the tone quality?

8. What is resonance?

9. What are sympathetic vibrations? Give some examples.

10. What is formant resonance? Name some musical instruments that employ formant resonance. Name some instruments that employ the harmonic theory of tone quality.

11. What is an Aeolian harp?

12. Be able to sketch two partials, then add them graphically. Conversely, be able to determine visually the partials in a complex wave.

13. Give some examples of noise. Does noise have an identifiable pitch? Does the speaking voice contain noise?

14. How does noise appear on an oscilloscope?

15. How can one illustrate the partials in a singing voice?

CHAPTER **5**

Beats and Combination Tones

5.1 Definition of a Beat

Two pure tones whose frequencies are 500 and 501 Hz when sounding together will move in and out-of-phase once per second. In other words, if they start in phase, they will reinforce one another; one-half second later they will be 180° out-of-phase and cancel one another; one-half second later they will be back in phase to begin the cycle again. This means that the intensity or loudness of the tone heard will increase and decrease once a second. This change in loudness is called a beat and its rate will be the difference in the two frequencies. For example, if 500 and 501 Hz are sounded together, one beat per second will be heard; if 500 and 510 Hz are sounded together, ten beats per second will be heard. If pure tones are sounding, the oscilloscope would picture a sine wave which varies in amplitude in a smooth, sine wave manner.

5.2 The Beat Tone

If the beat rate exceeds 20 per second, it is sufficiently rapid that it will sound like another tone. If, for instance, real tones of 400 and 500 Hz are sounding together, the first difference tone would have a beat rate of 500–400 or 100 per second, producing a 100 Hz tone. There are other combinations which would be heard, although not actually sounded. They are all combination tones whose frequencies are arrived at by adding or subtracting whole-number multiples of the real tones. The general formula is

$$f_s = nf_h \pm mf_l$$

f_s = frequency of the subjective or beat tones
f_h = frequency of higher real tone
f_l = frequency of lower real tone
m and n = whole number integers

If $f_h = 500$, $f_l = 400$, $m = n = 1$, then $f_s = 500 \pm 400 = 900$ or 100;
If $m = 2$ and $n = 1$, then $f_s = 2(400) \pm 500 = 800 \pm 500 = 1300$ and 300, and so on.

Naturally, only positive frequencies are considered since negative frequencies are meaningless. There are many names used to identify these tones: beat, subjective, resultant, summation, difference, imaginary, combination. In radio vernacular, heterodyne refers to beat production.

41

5.3 Practical Uses for Beats

There are many ways in which beats are employed in everyday life. The final adjustment in tuning a piano string is done with beats. Because of the low frequency, a man's fundamental pitch heard over the telephone is not transmitted by the telephone, but since the higher frequency partials are, the pitch heard is a beat tone produced by the interaction (beating) of adjacent partials. The correct pitch is heard therefore, even though it does not come out of the receiver. A pilot adjusts the propeller speeds for a multi-engine plane to zero beats; that is, they are revolving with exactly the same r.p.m. Some orchestral instruments produce fundamental pitches which are not actually sounded by the instrument, but result from a beating produced by adjacent partials.

Review Questions for Chapter 5. Beats and Combination Tones.

1. Define "beat." How is a beat produced? Is it a variation in the loudness or pitch?

2. When does a beat cease to be a beat and become a beat tone?

3. How can the beat rate be measured? How can the beat rate be calculated?

4. If two pure tones of frequencies 500 and 550 Hz are sounded together, be able to determine the frequencies of other combination tones, both summation and difference.

5. What other names are used when referring to beat tones?

6. In what practical ways are beats employed, musically and non-muscially?

CHAPTER 6

Stringed Musical Instruments

6.1 The Evolution of Stringed Instruments

The Lyre and Harp

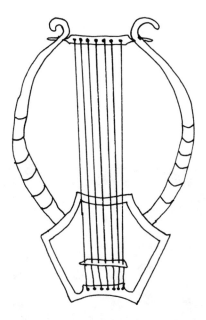

Figure 6.1. Lyre (Artist: Colleen Rayburn)

The lyre and harp are among the oldest instruments, documented in Mesopotamia c. 3000 B.C. Harps, nearly always plucked, had a soundboard perpendicular to the plane of the strings, unlike the zither or pianoforte which have parallel planes. Chromatic changes were made on the later harps with a hand adjusted device called a hook. It shortened the length of the string an appropriate amount, raising its pitch one semitone. At the beginning of the 19th century these hooks were replaced by foot-operated rotating discs from which two studs protruded. (Fig. 6.2.) They shortened the string and raised the pitch one or two semitones. One foot pedal was provided for each of the seven tones of the scale, allowing the harp to be played in any key.

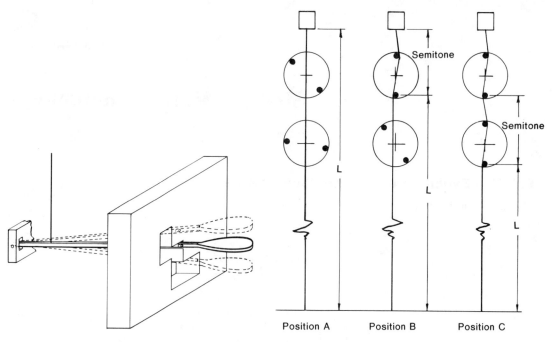

Figure 6.2A. Harp tuning pedal

Figure 6.2B. Harp tuning mechanism

Figure 6.3. Harp (Courtesy of Lyon and Healy, Inc.)

The harp usually has 46 strings made of gut, nylon and overwound steel for the low pitches, providing for a six and one-half octave range. Modern harps use strings of different colors to identify certain pitches, since there are no "landmarks" to assist the performer in locating the correct string. The piano provides these "landmarks" with its arrangement of black keys.

The Irish harp was played in one key since it had no tuning devices other than pegs and was not easily adjusted during performance.

The Aeolian harp was a wind blown string which produced an eerie, ghostly sound, vibrating at its fundamental frequency or its harmonics.

The Lute

Lute-like ancient stringed instruments were shown on Mesopotamian art works, c. 2000 B.C. They had a small round body, long neck, were fretted, had two strings with no tuning pegs, and employed a plectrum. The Lute was probably Arabic, invented c. 800–1100 A.D. The Renaissance and Baroque lute was one of the most popular of all instruments, c. 1600, and is being revived today.

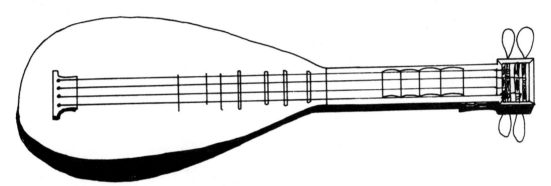

Figure 6.4. Chinese lute (Artist: Colleen Rayburn)

The Fiddle

The fiddle, a bowed lute, appeared c. 800 A.D. The body usually was made of bamboo, wood, or coconut, occasionally with taut lizard or snake skin serving as a soundboard. It had one or two silk strings tuned with iron pegs. The two strings were tuned to an interval of a fifth, with the bow hairs passing between the strings, sounding them simultaneously. It had no fingerboard; the fingers merely touched the string. The fiddle was a forerunner of the violin.

The Dulcimer

The dulcimer was of Persian and Iraqian origin, made with a shallow box resonator and eighteen quadruple brass strings tuned with pegs. The player struck the strings with light blade-ended sticks. The dulcimer was the forerunner of the harpsichord and pianoforte.

The Viol and Violin Families

During the 16th century, the viol family developed. The most visible characteristics of the true viols are the sloping shoulders of the body, the flat back, and the frets. Our contemporary bass viol is of the viol family, but has lost its frets.

Figure 6.5A. Violin (Courtesy of Conn, Artley, Scherl and Roth)

Figure 6.5B. Cello (Violoncello) (Courtesy of Conn, Artley, Scherl and Roth)

Figure 6.5C. Bass viol (Courtesy of Conn, Artley, Scherl and Roth)

The first great violin makers lived in Cremona, Italy, during the latter part of the 16th century, the most famous being Nicolo Amati (1596–1684), his student Antonio Stradivari (1655–1737), and Giuseppe Guarneri (1681–1742). Their violins, violas and celli have sold for fabulous sums and those that still remain are considred nearly priceless.

Various sized instruments compose the violin family: the violin, viola and cello. A fourth is the double bass which is closely related to the double bass viol. None of the violin family is fretted, nor is the contemporary double bass viol.

The Guitar Family

The guitar originated in the Orient around the 12th century, possessing the general characteristics of the plucked lute, except that its body was flat. In the 16th century the Renaissance guitar became a popular instrument and in the 17th century, the Baroque guitar found its place into serious music. The guitar, along with others of the same family (mandolin, ukulele, and banjo), has enjoyed great popularity during the past century as a "social" instrument, possibly because of its portability as well as its use in playing melodies as well as harmony. Unfortunately, most people do not know of the musical capabilities of the guitar and its stature in serious musical performance.

Of very recent years, particularly with the invention of the electric guitar, this instrument has attained a very prominent position in the entertainment field.

6.2 Law of Vibrating Strings

At the beginning of the 17th century, Mersenne experimented with a taut wire over one hundred feet long that vibrated so slowly he could count transverse vibrations and developed the following law of vibrating strings.

$$f = \frac{1}{2L}\sqrt{\frac{T}{m}}$$

f = frequency of the fundamental in Hz;
L = vibrating length in cm;
T = stretching force in dynes;
m = mass of 1 cm of the wire in gms.

Since most people who are not technically trained do not think in terms of dynes, centimeters and grams, the following formula is submitted which employs pounds and feet.

$$f = \frac{5.52}{2L}\sqrt{\frac{T}{m}}$$

f = frequency of the fundamental in Hz;
L = the vibrating length in feet;
T = the stretching force (tension) in pounds;
m = the weight of one foot of the wire or string.

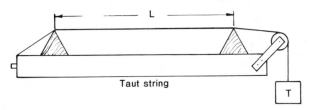

Figure 6.6. The law of vibrating strings

Example: The highest pitched steel string on a violin (E_5) was measured to have a vibrating length of 12.75″ (1.0625′); a diameter of 0.010″ which, from the wire tables would weigh 0.00027 pounds per foot, the frequency of $E_5 = 660$ Hz. Solving the above equation for tension,

$$T = \frac{m\ f^2}{\left(\dfrac{5.52}{2\ (L)}\right)^2} = \frac{(.00027)(660)^2}{\left(\dfrac{5.52}{2\ (1.0625)}\right)^2} = \frac{117.612}{6.75} = 17.43 \text{ pounds}$$

Note that from the formula, the frequency varies inversely with the length of the string, directly with the square root of the tension and inversely with the square root of the mass/unit length. In other words, to change pitch one octave either the length must be halved, or the tension must be quadrupled (since the square root of 4 is 2), or the mass/unit length must be quartered.

6.3 Construction of Strings

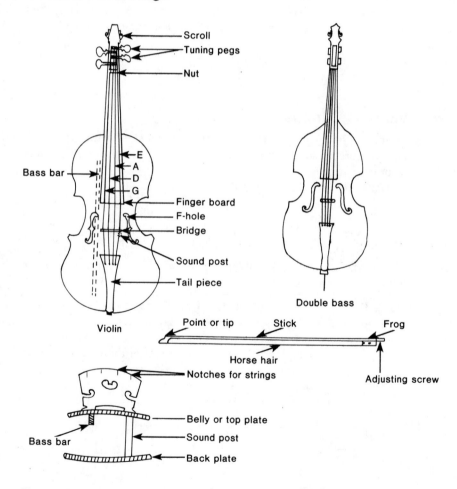

Figure 6.7. Parts of a stringed instrument (violin and bass viol) (Artist: Colleen Rayburn)

Among the more important considerations, a string must be strong (high tensile strength), not stretch out-of-shape (high elasticity), be chemically inert to prevent rusting or turning fingers green due to the salts in perspiration, be relatively inexpensive, unaffected by changes in humidity, tough enough to withstand abrasive action of sliding fingers. The materials which meet the above specifications are gut, stainless steel, nylon. For obvious reasons lead, copper, brass, and iron are among the materials which should be avoided.

There is a minimum tension which will permit a good tone quality. If the tension is too low, the tone quality is poor and the pitch will vary considerably with changes in the velocity of the bow. Therefore, since the maximum length of a string is fixed by the instrument, and a minimum tension is required, the only way left for the frequency of the string to be lowered to the required pitch is to increase its mass per unit length. We could employ a steel wire of greater diameter, but the stiffness would become so great that it would cut the fingers trying to depress it against the fingerboard. Instead, we employ a steel wire that can be adjusted to an appropriate tension, then increase its mass by overwinding it with another wire of suitable characteristics. This overwinding does not affect the tension but does increase the mass per unit length. Most stringed instruments employ overwound strings, at least for the low pitches. In the case of gut or nylon strings, this overwinding also provides additional protection against undue wear of the tension string.

6.4 The Bow

The bow, made of a thin shaft of wood, holds strands of horsehair taut much as an archer's bow holds the bow-string. Rosin is rubbed on the horsehair causing it to stick to the string. Many violinists believe that horsehair has little scales, like fish scales, which grab the string to make it vibrate. To check this belief, new, unused horsehair was examined under the microscope. No scales were found. The hair appears to be a small, smooth surfaced rod. If scales did exist, the friction against the string would wear them away. The "magic ingredient" is the rosin which causes the bow hair to stick to the string.

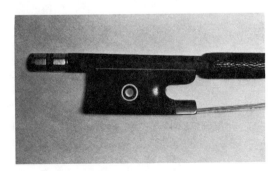 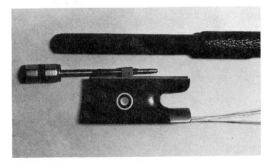

Figure 6.8. Bow frog showing hair tension adjusting mechanism (Photos by David Apple)

6.5 Producing the Tone

As the bow is drawn at a right angle to the string, it pulls the string aside until the static friction is overcome by the tension and the string is released only to stick again and be pulled aside. This stick-slip action occurs at the same frequency as the tone being heard.

To produce a good tone, the pressure of the bow on the string must be compatible with the bow velocity.

The bow makes contact with the string between the bridge and the bridge end of the fingerboard (Figure 6.7). Since the point of contact tends to locate the antinodes (maximum transverse motion) and prevents the development of a node (minimum transverse motion), the performer has some control over the partials developed, hence over the tone quality. (Figure 6.9.) Bowing near the bridge develops high frequency partials, whereas bowing away from the bridge (over the end of the fingerboard) minimizes these high frequency partials and develops those of lower frequency. A tone rich in high frequency partials might be described as harsh, nasal, metallic, or strident, whereas a tone devoid of these high frequency partials is less brilliant.

6.6 The Mute

The mute is a small device that clamps on the bridge much like a pinching clothespin (which works very well). This increases the mass of the bridge thereby reducing its lateral amplitude and thus the intensity of the tone. The high frequency partials are attenuated more than the low, so the quality of the tone is altered considerably making it more mellow. The more massive the mute, the greater the effect. With the attenuation of the higher partials, less sound energy is produced so the loudness of the tone is reduced.

6.7 Playing Harmonics

Touching the string lightly at a nodal point will cause it to vibrate in segments. The number of vibrating segments (loops) corresponds to the number of the partial sounding. For instance, if the string is vibrating with a single antinode (one segment), the first partial is sounded; with two antinodes (two segments), the second partial sounds. Fig. 6.9. The performer must avoid bowing or plucking the string at a nodal point which would force the string to vibrate where it must remain motionless, resulting in an unwanted tone.

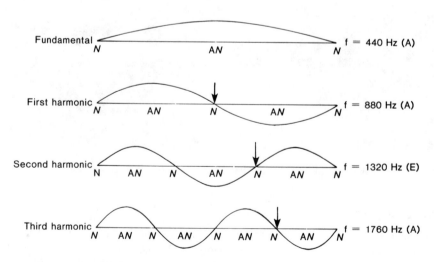

Figure 6.9. Harmonic operation of a taut string

If the string is plucked with the finger, producing a percussive tone, the initial deformation of the string is, of course, triangular. When the string is released, and allowed to vibrate, the high frequency partials quickly die out leaving a near sinusoidal type vibration.

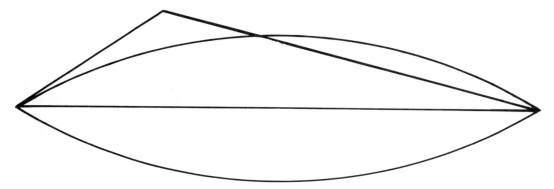

Figure 6.10.   Plucked string

Vibrations of the string are transmitted to the body of the violin through the bridge. The violin itself and the air cavity within the violin resonate the many formants and amplify the sound. The sound post, wedged between the belly (top plate) and back (back plate) of the violin under the bridge, serves two purposes: it helps support the pressure exerted on the belly by the taut string, and it connects the belly and back acoustically.

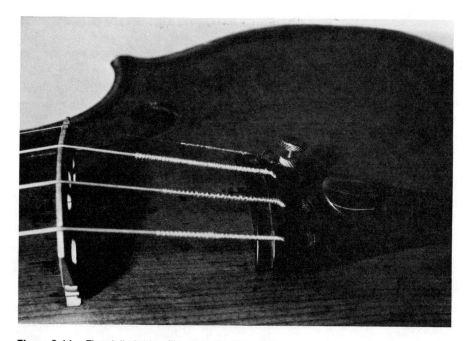

Figure 6.11.   The violin bridge (Photo by David Apple)

The F-holes (or C-holes) give vent to the rapid, though minute, changes in air pressure and contribute to the resonant characteristics of the instrument.

The bass bar is a strip of wood glued to the inside surface of the belly to support the left foot of the bridge and help distribute the vibrations over the surface of the belly, altering to some extent its vibrational patterns.

6.8 Tuning the Orchestral Strings

The violin, viola and cello are tuned to intervals of a Just fifth. (See Table 6-A.) The strings on a double bass, however, are so long it is difficult for the fingers to reach the positions necessary to play the scale tones. Also, the finger pressure required to "stop" the string is too great for many performers, because of the mass and tension (or stiffness), of the strings. Therefore, the double bass is tuned to intervals of a fourth which allows the performer to reach the correct pitches with the stronger fingers.

Table 6-A
Tuning the Orchestral Strings

Violin	Viola	Violoncello	Double Bass
E_5	A_4	A_3	G_2
A_4	D_4	D_3	D_2
D_4	G_3	G_2	A_1
G_3	C_3	C_2	E_1

6.9 Construction Materials

There are many myths surrounding the types of materials which must be used in making musical instruments, including the different woods, glue and varnish used to make the stringed instruments, and even the metals and woods to be used in manufacturing organ pipes.

If the material itself vibrates appreciably, such as the body of a violin or the thin metal bell of a French horn, the choice of material and its dimensions are critical. However, there are many instruments where the thickness or mass of the material is sufficiently great, such as the oboe, clarinet, or flute, that vibration of the material is so slight, its influence on the tone is imperceptible. Instead, the air column, the bore shape and the condition of the surface are the tonal determiners, not the tubing itself.

If this is true, what are the cirteria for the choice of materials? There are very practical reasons for the choice including the strength of the material, it's elasticity, workability, durability, freedom from warping, cracking, splitting, or wearing from abrasion, and the strength required for it to perform its function. Tubing for brass instruments or organ pipes must be malleable and lend itself to shaping and surfacing. In some cases, a material may be chosen which has a low coefficient of expansion so the changes in dimensions are not highly sensitive to temperature changes. Heat conductivity is another consideration: a metal flute conducts heat much better than a wood flute, so the temperature of the air column is subject to considerable variations with the accompanying changes in pitch.

Appearance is important also, so materials should be chosen which will be acceptable to the eye. People want an instrument to look like the prototype they know or remember. With the many new materials available, changes have been and will be made in the manufacturing of musical instruments.

Two of my graduate students, majoring in pipe organ performance, experimented with the construction of fiberglass-epoxy resin organ pipes. Inserting these pipes in an existing pipe organ, they produced a most acceptable tone, much to the astonishment of the organ builders who were at work at the time.

Already on the market are, among others, plastic wind instruments, plastic marimba bars. Many years ago, Dr. Joseph Maddy, in an attempt to find a more durable bass viol, developed a metal instrument which would withstand the rough treatment given by youngsters. Only one problem was encountered: it was too resonant. This was solved with an application of a tar substance to the inside surfaces of the instrument, much like the anti-rust coating given automobiles.

Very recently the bow hair, which formerly was selected with great care from a particular type of horse, and staggered in direction (see "Violin Bows") is being replaced with nylon filaments. The nylon is more rugged, less expensive, and works just as well as real hair.

There are countless other examples which could be sighted. I predict that modern technology will bring us not only many improved musical instruments utilizing the new materials already available and yet-to-be developed, but also completely new instruments, and all at a very much reduced cost. This field is expanding rapidly and the changes are exciting to contemplate.

6.10 The Evolution of Keyboard Stringed Instruments

Plucked keyboard instruments appeared in the second half of the 14th century. The clavichord, derived from the dulcimer by adding a keyboard, consisted of a small, shallow box provided with a thin soundboard to amplify the sound. The strings were stretched over one bridge from hitch pins to tuning pegs. Vertical brass hammers, called "tangents," were attached to each key and struck the string. The clavichord was a favorite instrument of J.S. Bach.

The spinet was a one-manual keyboard instrument in which the strings were plucked by quills, as were the virginal* and harpsichord, instead of being struck. The harpsichord was a keyboard instrument of the 16th to 18th centuries, similar in shape to the modern grand piano. On the larger harpsichords there are several strings for each key which produce higher or lower octaves. Different degrees of loudness were achieved by sounding more than one string at a time. In the 18th century, the harpsichord was replaced by the pianoforte, meaning soft-loud. The harpsichord is enjoying increased popularity in recent years.

The pianoforte, currently referred to as the piano, was so named because the velocity of the felt padded hammers could be controlled, sounding tones of varying degrees of loudness.

---

*The virginal is supposed to have been named after the virgin Queen Elizabeth, born in 1533. Since the virginal was mentioned several years before her birth, this is apparently a bit of levity.

6.11 The Piano

The piano is both a stringed instrument and a percussion instrument. Whether it be a grand or upright, the piano consists of the following principal parts: keys, hammer and dampers, strings, frame to support the string tension, bridge, sounding board, tuning pins, hitch pins, pedal mechanism, and the framework to hold it all together. Following is a brief description of each.
The keys

The standard keyboard has 88 keys, 12 to the octave. The white covering for the wood keys used to be made of ivory, but plastic now replaces the ivory as being more durable and less expensive.

6.12 Piano Hammers and Dampers

The hammer is made of felt-covered wood. The force with which it hits the strings is a function of the hammer's momentum (mass × velocity), so the mass is a critical factor, independent of the manner in which the piano is played, whereas the velocity is controlled by the performer, his only control of loudness. After the hammers have been used for a while, the felt is compressed so it is harder and makes a more harsh, "bar-room" sound. The felt can be rejuvenated by piercing it with needles to separate the fibers. If the piano technician wishes to "liven" a sound, he can do so by applying a hot iron to the felt which hardens it.

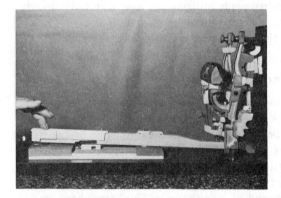 

Figure 6.12. Piano action with key depressed and released (Photos by David Apple)

Just before the hammer hits the string it is mechanically released from the key so the last quarter of an inch travel before it strikes the string results from its momentum. When the hammer bounces back it is caught and held by the "back check" so that it cannot rebound and strike the string again. If the key is now lifted a little, the repetition lever engages allowing for sounding a tone in rapid repetition. The "soft" pedal on the grand moves the action and keyboard, with all the hammers, sideways so that only two of the three strings are struck. In the upright piano this is accomplished by shifting the hammers closer to the strings, thereby reducing the velocity (momentum) and thus the loudness. When a key is depressed a felt damper is raised off the strings allowing the tone to continue sounding; it stops with the release of the key. If desired, this damper can be held off the strings by depressing the sustaining pedal, allowing the strings to vibrate freely.

6.13 The Piano Strings

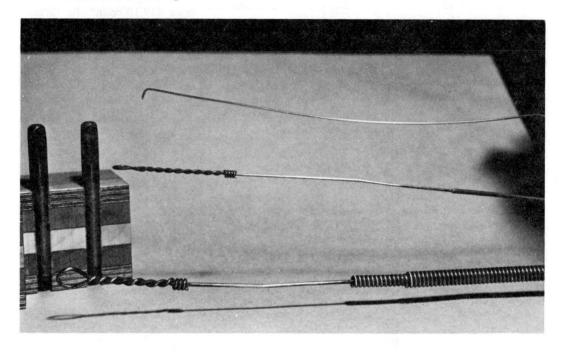

Figure 6.13. Piano strings and tuning pins (Photo by David Apple)

Except for the very low pitches, each tone requires two or three strings to produce the required tonal volume. Because of the greater amplitude and motion, the medium low pitches require only two strings, and the lowest tones but one string. It was determined empirically that the optimum tension per string to produce a good tone is about 150 pounds. Since there are approximately 230 strings in a piano, the total tension amounts to some 18 to 20 tons (36,000 to 40,000 pounds). Recalling the law of vibrating strings: $f = \dfrac{c}{2L}\sqrt{\dfrac{T}{m}}$, if the tension is maintained constant, the frequency must be determined by the length and the mass. If only the length were varied, a grand piano would have to be 22–26 feet long; 2.5 times as long as it actually is to produce the lowest tones, and the highest would be less than two inches in length. Therefore, the mass (diameter) of the highest strings is less than the middle register; below that the steel strings are overwound with copper or brass wire to increase their mass. The lowest are doubly overwound and approximately 3/16″ in diameter. Note that the tension is applied only to the steel core wire with the overwinding adding only to the mass.

Example: The highest note on a grand piano is C_8 = 4185.98 Hz. Each of the three strings measures 0.033″ (size 14) which weighs 0.002857 pounds per foot; the length measures 1.75″ (0.1458 feet). What tension is exerted on each of the three strings?

$$T = \frac{m\,f^2}{\left(\frac{5.52}{2L}\right)^2} = \frac{(0.002857)(4185.98)^2}{\left(\frac{5.52}{2(0.1458)}\right)^2} = \frac{50061.57565}{358.345} = 139.70 \text{ pounds each,}$$
or 419.10 pounds for three

6.14 The Piano Frame

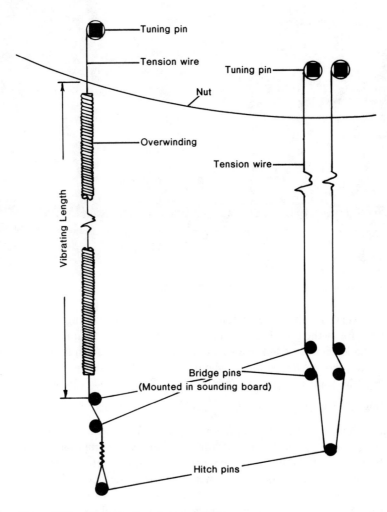

Figure 6.14.   The mounting of piano strings

The framework that holds the strings taut was made of wood until about 150 years ago when it was changed to cast iron to support the very great tension involved. This made for a more constant tension since cast iron is not susceptible to warping with changes in humidity and temperature. One end of the string is attached to a hitch pin mounted on one end of the cast iron frame, the other end wraps around the tuning pin which is driven into a hard maple pinblock mounted on the other end of the iron frame. Tuning is done with a tuning hammer (wrench) to vary the string tension.

A string, vibrating by itself, will produce a very weak tone needing amplification just as does a violin string. To accomplish this, as in the violin, a sounding board is mounted under the strings with contact being made where the strings cross the bridge. This sounding board is a thin, laminated panel, sometimes Sitka spruce or mahogany, about 3/16 to 3/8 of an inch thick. It is mounted under tension with a convex crown. Ribs are affixed to the panel to stiffen it and help maintain the crown. This sounding board vibrates and, because of its large area, radiates the sound and increases its volume. Occasionally, due to the drying of the wood, particularly in the winter time, and changes in temperature, the sounding board cracks. When this happens the sound goes dead much like a cracked bell. Major repairs or replacement are required. The design of the sounding board which will radiate fairly uniformly all frequencies produced by the piano, has been evolved empirically over many years and as yet is more of an art than a science.

6.15 The Piano Pedal Mechanism

Many pianos have but two pedals. On the left is the "soft" pedal, on the right the sustaining pedal. Some of the better pianos have a third pedal between the two mentioned, called a sostenuto pedal. When a key is depressed and the pedal is pushed down, the felt dampers for those will be held off the strings without affecting the other dampers. This permits the sustaining of one or a few tones while the vibrations of the others will be stopped immediately.

6.16 The Piano Body

This body of the piano is usually made of solid and laminated wood—usually poplar, birch, and beech. It is carved, painted or varnished in various ways to make the instrument strong and attractive. This "body" has little to do with the tone except for the top of a grand which can be opened partially to direct the sound towards the audience.

6.17 Tuning the Equally-tempered Instruments

With the appropriate equipment and considerable practice, it is possible for you to tune your own piano. The procedure is shown as follows.

The beat rates employed for securing equal temperament be calculated from the following:

Perfect 4th = 3*Fa − 4*Do
Perfect 5th = 3 Do − 2 Sol
Major 3d = 4 Mi − 5 Do
Major 6th = 3 La − 5 Do

$$5(174.16) − 4(220)$$
$$= 873.05 − 880 = \quad 6.95$$

*The coefficients refer to the number of the partial of the complex piano tones responsible for the best production.

These calculations are made for the range F_3 through E_4, using the standard pitch $A_3 = 220$ Hz.

One string of A_3 is tuned to a tuning fork. Then, one string of the other pitches is tuned correctly by employing beats. The remaining strings for a given pitch are then tuned to produce no beats with the first string.

Once all tones within the octave are tuned correctly, pitches of the other octaves are tuned to produce no beats with them.

E_5	=	329.63	A# =	233.08
D#	=	311.13	*A =	220.00
D	=	293.66	G# =	207.65
C#	=	277.18	G =	196.00
C	=	261.63	F# =	185.00
B	=	246.94	F =	174.61

Beats per second	Interval	
+6.95	3d	
−0.57	5th	
+0.89	4th	
−0.68	5th	
+7.93	6th	Check
+0.98	4th	
−0.74	5th	
+8.88	6th	Check
+1.12	4th	
+7.76	3d	Check
+0.82	4th	
−0.64	5th	
+0.94	4th	
+8.27	3d	Check
−0.69	5th	
+8.39	6th	Check
+1.07	4th	
+7.32	3d	Check

+ = Wide
− = Narrow

6.18 The Acoustic Guitar

Figure 6.15.   The acoustic guitar (Courtesy of Conn, Artley, Scherl and Roth)

The acoustic guitar is not sufficiently different in design and operation from the violin to warrant an elaborate discussion. The resonance comes from its hollow cavity and the instrument itself. Formerly, it used gut strings, but in 1946 nylon strings were adopted. Steel is used on the electric guitar. The instrument usually has a flat top and back. Since it is not bowed, the nut and bridge are straight across the top rather than curved as on a bowed instrument. The instrument is plucked or strummed with the fingers or a plectrum.

6.19 The Electric Guitar

Figure 6.16.   The electric guitar (Photo by Mark White)

The early electric guitar was an acoustical guitar with its body and/or cavity resonator equipped with a microphone to generate the electrical signal to be amplified. This method had its disadvantages. The microphone also responded to any percussive contact with the body of the instrument as well as to nearby sounds and conversations since it was sensitive to acoustical disturbances rather than to the motion of the string. Also, amplified tones easily produced acoustical feedback.

The next step in the evolution of the electric guitar was to apply a magnetic field to the vibrating metal string. As the string cut the magnetic field, a voltage was developed between the two ends, accurately representing the motion of the string, which then could be amplified. However, the impedance (resistance), of this single wire was extremely low, requiring an audio transformer to match the impedance to the amplifier input.

Any disturbance of a magnetic field, such as a steel string vibrating near the permanent magnet, produces a variation in the strength of that magnetic field. By wrapping a small permanent magnet with several thousand turns of fine copper wire, these variations in magnetic field produce a considerably increased variation in the voltage developed, like a transformer, which then may be amplified. These wrapped magnets had a very much greater impedance so a transformer normally is not required.

The placement of magnets along the length of the string will determine the tone quality. Examining the harmonic operation of a vibrating string, Fig. 6.9, one easily can see that by placing the magnet at the string's mid-length, a voltage will be developed reproducing the first partial (fundamental), 3d, 5th, and so on. This tone quality will be similar to a clarinet. By placing the magnet near the bridge, the high frequency partials will be developed (or the low frequency partials will be lessened) sounding much like an oboe. With the proper positioning of magnets, and choice of polarities, nearly any tone quality desired can be attained.

6.20 Tuning the Strummed Instruments

The open strings of the guitar family, like the orchestral strings, are tuned to Just pitches as shown in Table 6-B. Most casual performers tune the strings to the heard pitches, perhaps checking with a piano, tuning fork or pitch pipe.

Table 6-B
Tuning the Strummed Instruments*

	Guitar Family			
Spanish or Electric	Tenor or 4-string (acoustic)	Bass (electric)	12-string (strings in pairs)	
E_4	E_4	G_2	E_4	E_4
B_3	B_3	D_2	B_3	B_3
G_3	G_3	A_1	G_4	G_3
D_3	D_3	E_1	D_4	D_3
A_2			A_3	A_2
E_2			E_3	E_2

*There are many systems of tuning practiced, but these are probably the most usual.

Table 6-B—Continued

Mandolin	Ukulele	Banjo	5-string Banjo
E_5	A_4	A_4	G_4
A_4	E_4	D_4	D_4
D_4	C_4	G_3	B_3
G_3	G_4	C_3	G_3
			C_3

6.21 Unison Tuning of the Guitar

A more accurate way to tune a guitar than just described, is by "unison" tuning. To do this, the pitches produced by stopped strings (the string is depressed firmly against the fret), are then compared to the pitch produced by an open string. Unison pitches will be heard. Follow, step-by-step, the procedure shown in Fig. 6.17. This method of tuning has its limitations because the reference pitches are derived from fretted tones, which are tempered. Since the strings must be Just in intonation, the "harmonic" method of tuning is the most accurate.

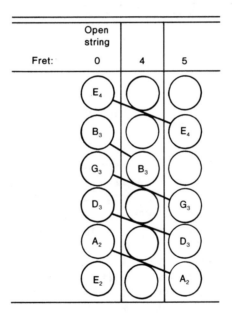

Figure 6.17. Unison tuning of guitar employing stopped strings

6.22 Harmonic Tuning of the Guitar

To tune the guitar with harmonics, set the pitch of the E-string, then follow the unison and octave tuning sequence shown in Fig. 6.18. Note that all tones are produced by sounding harmonics. Touch the string lightly over the fret indicated, then pluck the string. Faulty intonation, due to the imperfections of the strings, may be improved "by ear." Probably the best solution is to replace the strings.

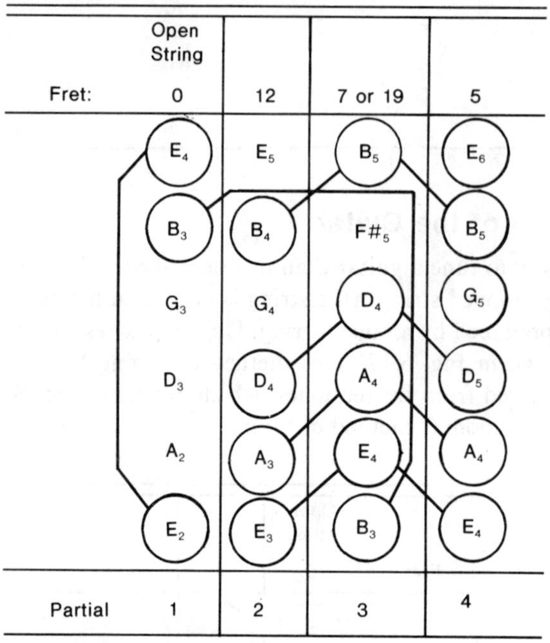

Fret:	Open String 0	12	7 or 19	5
	E_4	E_5	B_5	E_6
	B_3	B_4	$F\#_5$	B_5
	G_3	G_4	D_4	G_5
	D_3	D_4	A_4	D_5
	A_2	A_3	E_4	A_4
	E_2	E_3	B_3	E_4
Partial	1	2	3	4

Figure 6.18. Pitches employed for harmonic tuning of Spanish-electric guitar

Members of the guitar family are fretted instruments with fixed pitch relationships. Like the piano, if these instruments are to be in tune in every key, the frets must determine tempered pitches. Table 6-C lists the length of the vibrating portion of the strings on the Spanish-electric Guitar to provide for correct tempered intonation.

It should be mentioned that in the case of an acoustic guitar, the resonant characteristics of the instrument itself and its resonant cavity, determine to a large degree the tone quality produced. With the solid-bodied guitar, deriving its tone almost entirely from the motion of the string, the resonance of the instrument may have a slight, but minor effect on the tone quality, and the shape has no effect. For this reason, most electric guitars have solid bodies with no resonant chamber, though made to look like a guitar for sales appeal.

Table 6-C
The Spanish-electric Guitar
Fret Location for Tempered Intonation

Partial (Just)	Fret Number	Length of String Between Fret and Bridge in cm. (Tempered)
	0	63 (maximum length)
	1	59.46
	2	56.13
	3	52.98
	4	50.00
$\frac{L}{4}$ = 4th partial	5	47.20
	6	44.55
$\frac{2L}{3}$ = 3d partial	7	42.05
	8	39.69
	9	37.46
	10	35.36
	11	33.37
$\frac{L}{2}$ = 2nd partial	12	31.50
	13	29.73
	14	28.06
	15	26.49
	16	25.00
	17	23.60
	18	22.27
$\frac{L}{3}$ = 3d partial	19	21.02
	20	19.84
	21	18.73
	22	17.68

The special effects possible with an electric guitar are limited only to the engineer's inventiveness. With the nearly endless possibilities of electronic circuitry, the tone can be shaped, altered and controlled to produce striking effects, unattainable on the acoustic guitar, such as the wah-wah, fuzz tone, reverberation, phase-shifter, echo chamber, tremolo, and more. Many of the techniques presently employed in the production of electronic music can be, and are, employed in guitar controls.

Review Questions for Chapter 6. Stringed Instruments.

1. Be able to describe generally the evolution of stringed instruments.

2. Who are probably the three most famous violin makers? When and where did they live?

3. Be able to describe in general terms the violin, viola, cello and bass viol.

4. Name the parts of a stringed instrument.

5. What purpose does the "f" or "c" hole serve?

6. What two purposes does the sound post serve?

7. What is the law of vibrating strings? If each parameter is quadrupled, how much does the pitch change?

8. What methods are employed to adjust the mass of the string?

9. What actually happens as the bow is drawn across the string? What substance is applied to the bow hairs, and for what purpose?

10. Can an "A" string on a violin replace the "E" string? The "D" string? Why, or why not?

11. What two changes in a violin tone does the "mute" produce? Why?

12. When the performer plays "harmonics," where must the finger touch the string to sound the pitch of the 2nd partial? The 5th partial? Is a node or antinode produced where the finger lightly touches the string?

13. When a string is "plucked" with a finger, what is this method of playing called? Is it a percussive tone or not?

14. On what stringed instruments are frets used? What is the purpose of the fret?

15. What factors determine the material to be used in making a musical instrument?

16. Of what material is the bow hair made? Is there any other material that can be used?

Keyboard Stringed Instruments

1. Be able to describe generally the evolution of keyboard stringed instruments.

2. How is the sound produced on a harpsichord? Does the manner of depressing the key affect the loudness of the tone?

3. The complete name for a piano is "pianoforte." What does this name mean?

4. What control does a pianist have on the loudness of the tone produced? (Remember, the key is disconnected from the hammer just before the moment of impact.)

5. Is the piano a percussive or non-percussive instrument?

6. The soft pedal on a piano can work in two ways. What are the mechanisms?

7. How are the different pitches on a piano obtained? (Refer to the law of vibrating strings.) Which factors are varied, which are constant?

8. What is the approximate tension on a single piano string? What is the approximate total string tension on a piano?

9. What does overwinding a piano string do? Is this overwinding under tension, or is it just the core string?

10. Where, along the length of a piano string, does the hammer strike? Why?

11. Do all of the tones on a piano employ the same number of strings? Why?

12. A very essential part of a piano vibrates sympathetically to amplify the sound. What is it called? To prevent this part from cracking, does it require a very dry atmosphere, or should the air be humidified? If this part cracks, is the tone impaired? Why?

13. What supports the tremendous tension exerted by the piano strings? Of what material is it made?

14. How does a piano technician tune a piano? Is there an electronic instrument to assist in this job? Describe.

The Guitar

1. Of what materials are the strings of an acoustic guitar made? An electric guitar?

2. Describe the evolution of the electric guitar.

3. To what intonation are the frets tuned—tempered or Just?

4. To what intonation are the strings tuned—tempered or Just?

5. What is meant by "unison tuning" and "harmonic tuning" of a guitar?

CHAPTER 7

Wind Instruments

7.1 The Evolution of Woodwind Instruments

The Flute

Probably the first flute was discovered accidentally when hollow cane stalks were blown across their ends, making an interesting sound. Primitive people were very superstitious and this "magic" was felt to be the voice of the spirits. These end-blown instruments are known as vertical flutes and seen today in the recorder.

Vertical flutes, played by hunters to lure the game, were first recorded in the 4th millenium, B.C. In Egypt the simple vertical flute can be traced back to the centuries before 3000 B.C. Due to the large ratio of length to diameter, the lowest tone was the second partial, the first partial (fundamental) being so weak that the instrument overblew the octave. Egyptian cane flutes were a yard long and a half-inch in diameter, with six finger holes near the lower end. One had a thumb hole in the back. Flutes were used in ritual music c. 2600 B.C.

Whistle flutes had a mouthpiece to direct the air against the hole's edge. Globular flutes were made of hollow fruit, then coconut shells with mouth and finger holes. Later, in Babylonia, they were made of clay. Our contemporary descendant is known as the ocarina or "sweet potato." Bone flutes, or nose flutes, were blown through the nostrils instead of the mouth. Double and triple flutes were used by the Tibetans.

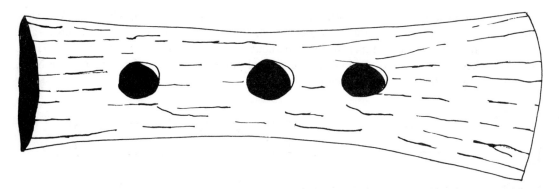

Figure 7.1. Vertical bone flute (Artist: Colleen Rayburn)

Pan pipes were sets of cane tubes, stopped at their lower ends, tied together in raft or bundle-form, and blown across the upper ends in the manner of vertical flutes.

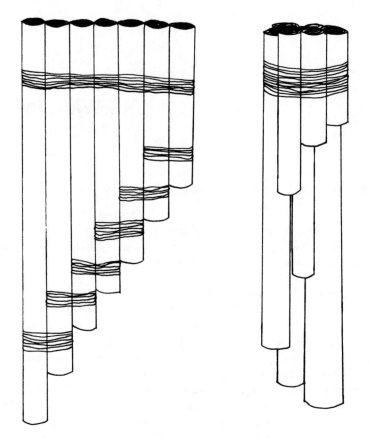

Figure 7.2.   Pan pipes, raft form (left) and bundle form (Artist: Colleen Rayburn)

The recorder appeared in the 14th century A.D. It was an end-blown whistle flute with a cylindrical bore. Later, during the Baroque period, the bore became conical with the largest diameter near the mouth, then tapering down to about one-half the diameter at the far end. Holes were positioned over its length to produce the desired pitches. Families of recorders were built, varying in length from about nine to eighty inches.

Figure 7.3.   The recorder (Artist: Colleen Rayburn)

By the last quarter of the 18th century, interest in the recorder had nearly disappeared, only to regain its popularity within recent years. Its beautiful tone is flute-like but incapable of being played loudly, so it normally is used in small, intimate groups.

The Double-reed Family

The earliest double-reed instruments, dating from about 3000 B.C., were double oboes, constructed in pairs with two tubes of different length, bound together and blown simultaneously. The longer tube sounded a drone and the shorter tube was provided with holes to play a melody. They were made of cane about two feet long and one-half inch in diameter, with a double reed or coarse grass mouthpiece. In ancient Egypt many double instruments have been excavated.

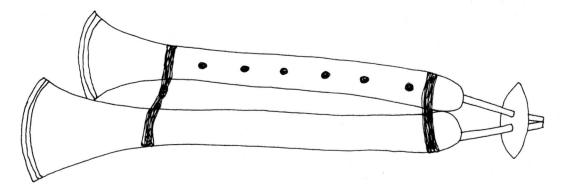

Figure 7.4. Double oboe (Indian) (Artist: Colleen Rayburn)

For a period of time the cane instruments were replaced by slender silver tubes with four fingerholes. All over the world, pipers used double oboes. There is mention of the funeral pipers playing when Christ restored life to Jairus's apparently dead daughter.

The bagpipe usually has several reed-pipes attached to a bladder or windbag that is held under the arm(s) to produce air pressure which causes the single or double reeds to sound. The player keeps the windbag inflated by blowing air into it through a slender tube, or by operating bellows with the arms.

One or two of the reed-pipes are equipped with holes to play melodies; several longer pipes produce drone tones. The bagpipe was known at least by the first century, A.D. Writings say that the Roman Emperor, Nero, played the bagpipes.

The late medieval ancestors of the oboe were known as shawms, becoming known as oboes during the latter part of the 17th century. The French developed the oboe from the shawms, calling it hautbois, meaning "high wood," or, according to some authorities, "loud wood."

The Cor Anglais (English horn), an alto oboe, was originally curved in shape which possibly explains the name. It assumed a straight form in the 19th century.

The bassoon, the bass of the double reed family, was known in the 16th century. It came from the Dulcion family. It has a conical bore and a large double reed. Due to its long length, the instrument is bent back on itself like a hairpin, with the sound issuing from the top end, the reed attached to the crook, a narrow, curved, metal tube. The contra-bassoon is the lowest pitched member of this family, having a length of over sixteen feet, with a construction similar to the bassoon.

The Single Reed Family

The clarinets are constructed with cylindrical tubes, closed at the upper end, but near this end is a small lateral opening covered by a single reed. The primitive ancestors of the clarinet were made of cane, appearing on a relief as a double clarinet c. 2700 B.C. The forerunner of the clarinet was known as a chalumeau, evolving into the clarinet during the 18th century as a result of work by John Denner. Mozart used the clarinets in some of his later compositions.

The Saxophone, invented by Adolph Sax of Brussels in 1840, had a single reed like the clarinets, but a conical bore like the oboe though greater in diameter. It was made of metal. There are six sizes in the saxophone family today, providing a wide range of pitch and timbre. Because the saxophone blends well with the woodwind and brass instruments, it is used principally in bands.

7.2 Open and Closed Tube Resonance

An air column will transmit longitudinal waves which are reflected from the end whether it be open or closed. If a pure tone is introduced into an open end, and its reflection produces a standing wave within the tube, the tube is resonant to this frequency. At the open end of a tube the air is free to vibrate so the amplitude of vibration will be maximum, or an antinode. A tube, open at both ends, will have an antinode at each end with, of course, a node centered between them. This is the fundamental resonant frequency of the open tube where the tube length is ½λ. Maintaining antinodes at the open ends, it is possible for the tube to resonate higher frequencies with more nodes and antinodes. Figure 7.5 shows the amplitudes within an open tube for the fundamental (solid line) and the first two harmonic overtones.

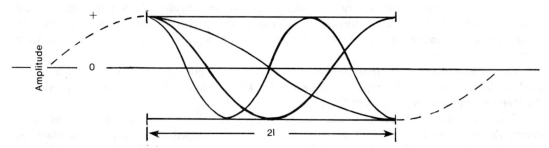

Figure 7.5.   Open tube resonance

A tube, open at one end and closed at the other, will resonate with an antinode at the open end and a node at the closed end where the gas particles are not free to vibrate. This is the fundamental resonant frequency of a closed tube where the tube length is ¼λ. Maintaining an antinode at the open end and a node at the closed end, it is possible for the tube to resonate higher frequencies with more nodes and antinodes. Note in Figure 7.6 the fundamental and the first two harmonic overtones. Only the odd numbered partials are resonated in the closed tube, where both even and odd numbered partials are resonated in the open tube. Also, a closed tube of length "l" resonates the same frequency as an open tube of length 2l.

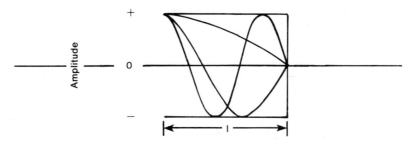

Figure 7.6. Closed tube resonance

A hole, cut in the side of a resonant column, develops an antinode at that point. (Fig. 7.7.) If the hole has a fairly large diameter, it would be the equivalent of sawing the instrument off at the hole, thus reducing the length of the resonant column and raising the pitch a predetermined amount.

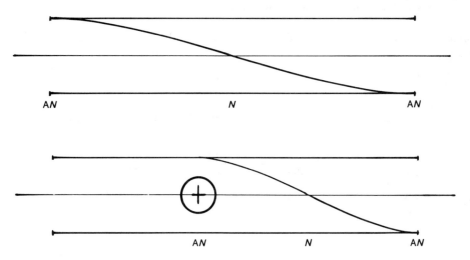

Figure 7.7. Hole in tube develops antinode, raising pitch

7.3 Determining the Resonant Frequency

A rough determination of the fundamental resonant frequency of a closed tube may be made by setting its length equal to one-fourth the wavelength sought. To refine this, there are two factors which need to be taken into consideration, (1) the velocity of sound which is a function of temperature and (2) the "end effect" of the single, open end. The basic formula: $f = \frac{v}{\lambda}$ where $v = 1054 + 1.1 \ T°_F$ so $f =. \frac{1054 + 1.1 \ T}{\lambda}$.

A wave within a tube can not "spread out" instantly at the open end (the end effect), so acoustically the tube length extends beyond the open end a small amount. This amount is a function of the diameter so 0.3 d′ must be added to the actual measured tube length, "l," which will be called the acoustical length, "L." See Fig. 7.8.

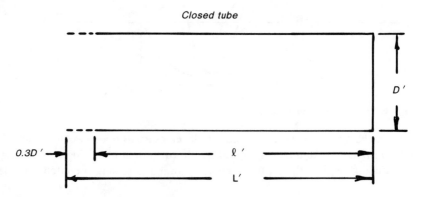

Figure 7.8.   End correction for closed tube

The fundamental frequency of a closed tube of actual length l′, and diameter d′, is given by the following relationship.

$$f = \frac{1054 + 1.1 \; T°F}{4 \; (l' + 0.3 \; d')}$$

If a closed tube has an actual length of l′, a diameter of l″ (which is .0833′) and the temperature is 70°F,

$$f = \frac{1054 + 1.1 \; (70)}{4 \; [1.0 + (0.3 \times 0.0833)]} = \frac{1131}{4 \; (1 + 0.025)} = 275.85 \; \cdot \; \cdot \; \cdot \; Hz.$$

The tube, open at both ends, would have an end correction applied to each open end so the acoustical length L = 1.0 + 0.6 d′

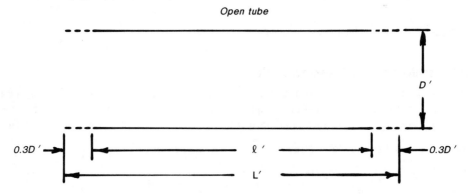

Figure 7.9.   End correction for open tube

$$f = \frac{1054 + 1.1 \ T°F}{2 \ [l' + (2 \times 0.3d')]}$$

$$f = \frac{1054 + 1.1 \ (70)}{2 \ [l' + (0.6 \times 0.0833)]} = \frac{1131}{2 \ (1 + 0.05)} = 538.57 \ \cdots \ H$$

7.4 Types of Bores

There are four principal types of bores employed in the manufacture of wind instruments—many instruments using two or three types: they are cylindrical, conical, logarithmic or exponential, or Bessel. The flare or bell on most instruments serves as a megaphone and amplifies by improving the radiation of the sound.

A closed conical tube operates like an open pipe and resonates all partials. Examine the illustrations, Fig. 7.10, where the three pipes all resonate the same fundamental frequency.

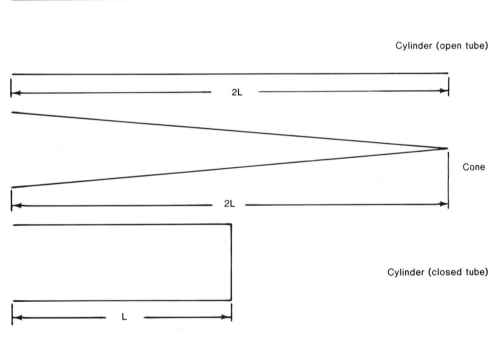

Figure 7.10. Three pipes resonating the same fundamental frequency

It might be appropriate here to point out that the air temperature within a wind instrument is higher than outside the instrument. A metal instrument radiates heat better than one made of wood. Since the velocity of sound is directly proportional to the temperature, the higher the temperature, the higher the pitch. Actual measurements show the temperature, after continuous playing, inside a metal flute is 79°F; inside a wood clarinet is 83°F, when the ambient temperature is 70°F. The clarinet playing 440 Hz initially, will sound about 446 Hz when warmed up.

The Sound Sources: Vibrating Reed or Reeds, an Edge Tone, or uzzing Lips

Vibrating Reed(s)

Perhaps you have blown between two pieces of paper, or blown a blade of grass held between your two thumbs to produce a loud squawk. This vibration is not unlike that produced by a vibrating reed.

Reed instruments employ a fine grained cane called Arundo Donax that resembles bamboo and grows best in France. To make a reed for any of the reed instruments, a longitudinal slice of cane is shaped to the correct size, and in the case of the double reeds is folded back on itself and bound with thread to a tiny brass tube, or a mandrel, then scraped to a tapered end and cut off to form two reed blades. The clarinet reed is thinned to a thickness of .0035″ to .0042″ for the samples measured. The thinner the reed, the easier it is to play and the reedier the quality. Each of the two reeds for the oboe is thinned to a thickness of .0036″ to .00425″; the English horn to about .0037″; the bassoon from .0065″ to .0112″. Compare these to the thickness of a sheet of 20-pound typing paper which is .004″.

When the reed is affixed to the instrument, its vibrations cause the column of air to resonate. The reed is very tightly coupled to the resonant cavity which determines the reed's vibration frequency.

The Edge Tone

If a jet of air with sufficient velocity strikes a sharp edge, instead of just splitting the air stream, the stream wobbles or vibrates back and forth producing an audible tone. If this vibration source is coupled to a resonant tube, the frequency of the edge tone will be the same as one of the resonant frequencies of the air column, the mode determined by the velocity of the air jet. Jumping to a higher frequency is called overblowing. The edge tone is employed in producing tones on a flute, organ pipe, the recorder, the whistle and even the bottle or jug.

The Buzzing Lips

If the lips are drawn back and air forced between them, a buzz is produced. The air pressure within the oral cavity increases until the lips are forced to part. When this happens, the air pressure drops immediately, allowing the lips to close and build up the pressure again. The frequency of the buzz is a function of the tension of the lips, the length of the vibrating portion, the tissue characteristics (mass), and the air pressure. The lip-buzz is tightly coupled to the instrument's resonant column frequencies, so the instrument determines the buzz frequency.

7.6 Woodwind Instruments: Flute and Piccolo, Clarinet, Saxophone, Oboe, English Horn, Bassoon

The Flute and Piccolo

Figure 7.11. Flute (Courtesy of Conn, Artley, Scherl and Roth)

Figure 7.12. Piccolo (Courtesy of Conn, Artley, Scherl and Roth)

The flute is an open tube with a cylindrical bore having a pitch range from C_4 to approximately C_7. The tone quality of the low pitches is reasonably complex but becomes more pure as the pitch ascends and/or the intensity decreases. The length of the air column is 23.75″. It is held horizontally and the tone is produced by blowing against the far edge of the mouthpiece hole. Eddies are developed which act as a piston in driving the resonant cavity. The efficiency of tone production is dependent almost entirely on the direction, shape, and velocity of the air jet. Only that portion of the jet which impinges upon the edge of the hole contributes to the tone. The portion of the jet which spreads wider than the aperture causes a breathy quality, and the performer will have difficulty sustaining a tone for a prolonged period due to the inefficiency of tone production.

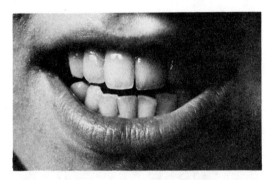

Figure 7.13. Jet-forming parts: teeth and lips (Photo by David Apple)

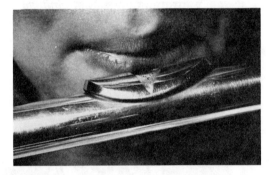

Figure 7.14. Flute air-jet, low pitch, well formed (Photo by David Apple)

Figure 7.15. Low pitch, jet too wide, producing breathy tone (Photo by David Apple)

The flutist can check the placement of this jet by cooling the mouthpiece with ice water, drying it, then observing the moisture condensation pattern produced by the jet.

The incisors and lips affect the shape the direction of the air jet. Frequently malformed incisors, or a space between them, makes the production of a good tone difficult or impossible. It is difficult for the flutist with a breathy or noisy tone to sustain it for prolonged periods since much of the breath is being used to produce noise with less going into the production of the tone. The vibrato can be produced at the larynx, but normally with the diaphragm, which causes a periodic change in jet velocity and therefore is principally an intensity vibrato.

The piccolo is a miniature flute. The older instruments were built in the key of D-flat, but the contemporary piccolos are one-half the flute length, hence one octave higher in pitch, and are built in the key of C, so are non-transposing.* Its tone is very shrill and piercing.

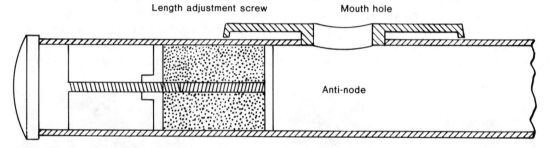

Figure 7.16.   The flute mouthpiece.

The Clarinet and Saxophone

Figure 7.17.   Clarinet (Courtesy of Conn, Artley, Scherl and Roth)

The clarinet consists of a cylindrical pipe made of wood, ebonite, metal, or plastic. The most usual clarinet in current use is built in the key of Bb, although the A clarinet is not uncommon. It uses a single bamboo reed, Figure 7.18, overblows only the odd numbered partials so the register key raises the pitch an octave and a fifth (12th) rather than the octave (8th) as with the oboe or flute.

*Transposing Instruments: Various of the orchestral instruments are built in keys other than "C," the piano pitch. As examples, the clarinet is usually built in B-flat, occasionally in A; the English horn is built in F; the saxophone in B-flat and E-flat. An instrument built in the key of B-flat reads "C" on the staff, but sounds the piano pitch, B-flat; built in F, reads "C" but sounds "F." In other words, when the instrument plays a "C" in the music, it will sound the piano pitch of the key in which it is built. This is very confusing not only for the performer, but also to the conductor who must mentally transpose each to determine the pitches which should be played. It has been necessitated, however, because the early instruments were built with differing fundamental pitches, and remain unchanged. Admittedly, this procedure is antiquated, but still persists!

When the reed is vibrating correctly, the two corners move in phase. However, if the reed is blown incorrectly, or it there is a slight split or imperfection in the feathered end, a "goose note" or "squawk" is produced which is about an octave higher in pitch, very unpleasant to hear and very unwanted by the performer.

When this happens, the two corners of the reed are moving 180° out-of-phase. This may be observed with a stroboscopic light. An almost imperceptable lateral cut with a razor blade, about 1/8th to 3/16th of an inch from the end will encourage a lateral type vibration and discourage the unwanted torsional vibration.

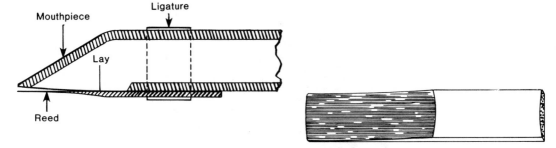

Figure 7.18. Clarinet mouthpiece and reed

The saxophone is a metal instrument with a clarinet-like mouthpiece and reed, yet has a large diameter conical bore. A complete family of saxophones exists, providing a wide range of pitch and timbre. It is a very popular instrument in dance bands and has found its way into the symphony orchestra and bands.

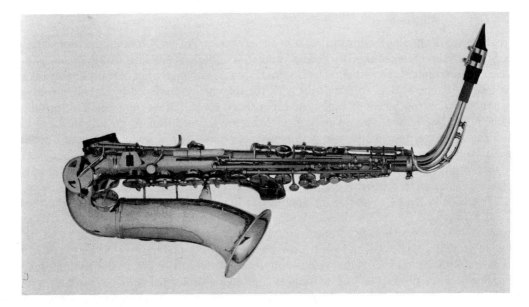

Figure 7.19. Saxophone (Courtesy of Conn, Artley, Scherl and Roth)

The Oboe, English Horn and Bassoon

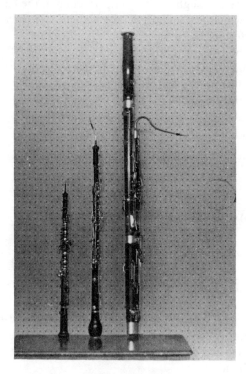

Figure 7.20.   The double reed family. Left to right: oboe, English horn, bassoon.

These are the double reed instruments of the orchestra. An early form of the oboe dates from the middle of the 17th century. Its bore is conical, it is built in the key of C and thus is a non-transposing instrument. The pitch range is from Bb_3 to G_6 although until recently the lowest keyed tone was B_3. It operates as an open tube with the tone being produced by a double reed which consists of two narrow pieces of cane bound to a short, conical brass tube which in turn fits into the end of the instrument. The tip ends of the reeds are scraped thin over a length of 1/4 to 3/8 of an inch in length. Frequently, a very thin piece of animal skin is wrapped around a portion of the reeds to prevent any possible leakage of air at the sides. The reeds vibrate, much like a clarinet reed, except that they both move and in opposition. You may have blown through a soda straw, flattened at the end, to produce a tone of "interesting" quality. This is much the same as an oboe reed. The oboe reed has no stationary mouthpiece like the clarinet against which the reed can beat. It is roughly 5/16 inch wide with a separation of perhaps 1/32″. This very small aperture does not allow for the passage of much air, so the oboist has the problem of using up the air stored in his lungs. Some oboists have learned the technique of maintaining the air pressure in the oral cavity with the tongue so the tone continues while he inhales or exhales through his nose. This allows for the production of a continuous tone over a prolonged period of time, perhaps five minutes or so, until the lack of blood circulation in the lips forces him to stop for a moment. Many times the audience, unaware of this "trick," gasps for breath while the oboist breathes merrily along!

The oboe reed is very sensitive and invariably is made and adjusted by the artist himself. The least bit of moisture between the reeds may cause the reed to stop vibrating or produce a gurgling effect. This moisture must be removed either by "kissing" the reed or by removing the reed from the instrument and blowing it out backward.

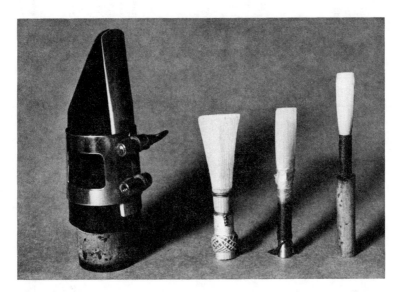

Figure 7.21. Clarinet reed and mouthpiece, bassoon, English horn and oboe reeds (Photo by David Apple)

The English horn is an alto oboe, larger and sounding pitches a fifth lower than the oboe. It is a transposing instrument, being built in the key of F. The reed, much like the oboe reed except being larger, fits on the end of a little tube, the crook, which is bent back towards the player's mouth, and fits in the upper end of the instrument. The lower end of the instrument, the bell, is pear shaped which serves as a resonant cavity, softening the tone quality.

The Bassoon, the bass of the double reed family, is so long the 100″ (8 1/3′) sound column is bent back on itself. The reed, much wider than that used by the English Horn, fits on the end of the crook—a narrow, metal, curved tube, which in turn connects to the instrument. The bore is conical. The tone quality is mellow and is used frequently for pastoral, melodic passages. Its range is from B^b_1 up to D_5. A version twice as long as the bassoon, the contrabassoon, sounds about one octave lower than the bassoon.

7.7 The Evolution of Brass Instruments

The earliest so-called trumpets, originating in the Neolithic age, did not produce a sound, but rather were used as megaphones, cut from a hollow branch or large cane stalk. Speaking into this tube produced a distorted sound and frightened the evil spirits. Then it was discovered that by buzzing the lips at one end, one or two blaring tones were produced.

Table 7-A
Woodwind Instruments

Name	Sound Source	Resonant Column	Concert (piano) Pitch Range	Transposing	Comments
Flute family					
Flute	Edge tone	23.75″ × .75″ essentially cylindrical	C_4–C_7	Non-transposing; built in C (G-flutes less usual)	Overblows all partials; velocity of air jet, which is perpendicular to flute axis, determines harmonic sounded.
Fife	Edge tone				Old military instrument
Recorder	Edge tone				Old form of flute; blown through mouthpiece in end; regained popularity in 20th century.
Piccolo	Edge tone	One-half length of flute	One octave higher than flute	Contemporary piccolo is non-transposing, built in C.	Very high pitched, with penetrating tone.
Oboe family					
Oboe	Double reed	Conical	Bb_3–G_6	Non-transposing; built in C.	Early forms of double reed instruments date from c. 3000 B.C.; end is bell shaped. Produces a pastoral, nasal quality.
English Horn	Double reed, connected to instrument with a crook (a narrow curved metal tube)	Conical	E_3–A_5	Transposing; built in F (plays C, sounds F a fifth lower).	Pearshaped bell alters quality of lowest pitches.
Bassoon	Double reed, connected to instrument with a short angled metal tube.	8′ conical tube, doubled back on itself	Bb_1–Bb_5	Non-transposing	Frequently plays pastoral solo passages; humorous effects produced by staccato performance earned the name "Clown of the orchestra."
Contrabassoon	Double reed, similar, but larger than bassoon	16′ long, conical, doubled on itself four times	One octave lower than bassoon Bb_0–Eb_3	Non-transposing	Large, heavy, held vertically, resting on floor.
Clarinet	Single cane reed	Basically cylindrical with slightly flared bell. Functions as a closed tube, overblowing the odd partials	D_3–G_6	Transposing; built in Bb (plays C, but sounds Bb one whole tone lower). Less usual, built in A and in Eb	Nearly the same length as flute (open tube, but sounds approximately one octave lower because of being a closed tube). Made of wood, ebonite or metal.
Saxophone	Single reed similar to clarinet reed.	Conical	Ab_3–Eb_6(Sop) Db_3–Ab_5(Alto) Ab_2–Eb_5(Tenor) Db_2–Ab_4(Bar)	Transposing: the most usual are Bb (soprano); Eb (alto); Bb (tenor); Eb (baritone)	A family of hybrid instruments invented by Adolph Sax c. 1840.

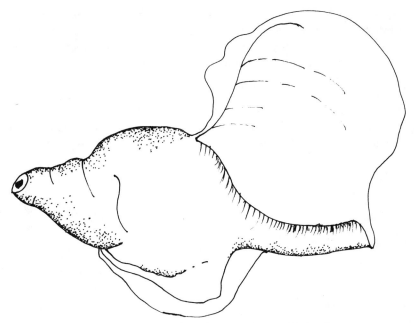

Figure 7.22.   Shell trumpet (Conch shell) (Artist: Colleen Rayburn)

Primitive man used large conch shells and elephant tusks as trumpets. Then, tubular trumpets evolved which sometimes were made of clay with a gourd serving as the bell. Oriental copper trumpets up to sixteen feet in length were too long and heavy to be placed without resting the end on the ground, much like the Alphorn in Switzerland, or the long wooden trumpets played at Rumanian funerals today. An early offshoot of the instrument is the transverse trumpet with a mouth-hole on the side.

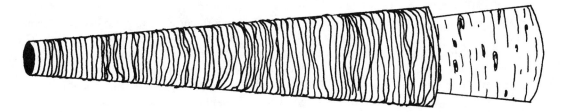

Figure 7.23.   Primitive trumpet (Artist: Colleen Rayburn)

Figure 7.24.   Straight cornet (Artist: Colleen Rayburn)

In the 16th century a fingerhole horn was developed called the serpent. It was a double bass of the cornet family. The snake-like shape was used to provide length to sound the low pitches, yet enable the performer to reach the six holes in the tubing. It was made of leather covered wood and had an ivory or bone mouthpiece like the higher pitched members of its family.

Keyed trumpets, bugles and French horns were developed during the eighteenth century. They had holes in the tubing much like a flute, sometimes covered with crude, keyed pads. All keyhorns were finally replaced by valved instruments in the 19th century. Before employing valves, four trumpets were required, with their four harmonic series, to the sound the lower register pitches of the chromatic scale. Valves made the single instrument into several. Both piston and rotary valves were used.

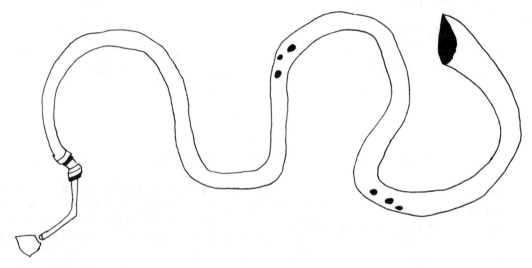

Figure 7.25.   Serpent (Artist: Colleen Rayburn)

The post horn, essentially a bugle, was equipped with piston valves producing an instrument with a less brilliant tone quality than the trumpet. The modern cornet came into being in France in 1825. It was a little shorter and wider, with a larger portion of its length of conical shape. The flugelhorn, originally a valved bugle, is of the cornet family but has a heavier tone quality.

Very rapidly the construction and refinement of "brass" instruments took place, providing a variety of pitch and quality ranges. These include the euphonium, baritone, slide and valve trombones, bass tuba and more recently, the helicon (Sousaphone).

7.8 Brass Instruments: Trumpet, Cornet, French Horn, Trombone, Tuba

The trumpet, used in orchestras, is a transposing instrument, usually built in the key of B-flat (like the clarinet). The cornet, used principally in bands, resembles the trumpet but with a less brilliant tone quality.

The mouthpieces of the trumpet, cornet, trombone and tuba are all cup-shaped (Fig. 7.28) and provide the necessary configuration to easily produce the buzz which initiates the sound. The interior shape of the cup determines to some extent the development of high frequency partials—the brilliance of the tone quality.

Concert (piano) pitches shown.

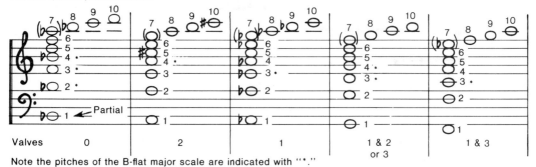

Valves   0   2   1   1 & 2 or 3   1 & 3

Note the pitches of the B-flat major scale are indicated with "•."

Figure 7.26. Trumpet valve combinations to produce harmonic series indicated

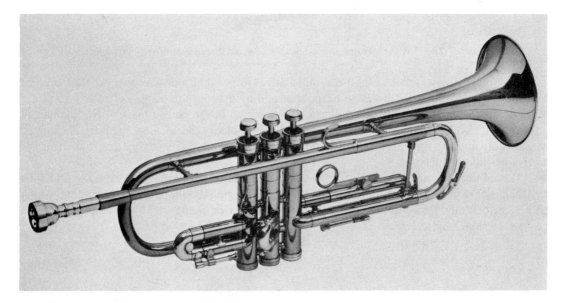

Figure 7.27. Trumpet (Courtesy of Conn, Artley, Scherl and Roth)

The horn (usually called French horn to prevent confusion with English horn, a woodwind), is a brass instrument, normally built in the key of F. Its conical tubing is a little over 12′ in length which winds in a tight spiral terminating with an exponential bell. The mouthpiece is unlike that employed by the trumpet in that its interior shape is conical with no sharp angles to develop high frequency partials, Fig. 7.28, which assists in the production of a mellow tone. The diameter of the bore is quite small at the mouthpiece end and very gradually increases over its length. This small diameter encourages the overblowing of the higher harmonics—the fundamental (pedal tone) cannot be played.

The quality of the French horn blends well with woodwind as well as brass instruments so it is sometimes referred to as a member of the woodwind family. The English hunting horn is a valveless horn quite similar in construction to the French horn.

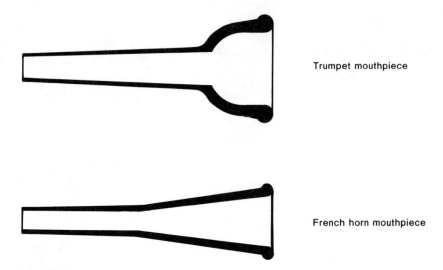

Figure 7.28.   The trumpet cup-shaped mouthpiece and the conical French horn mouthpiece

Most present-day French horns use a rotary valve (rather than a piston valve like the trumpet) but this valve accomplishes the same purpose of adding appropriate lengths of tubing to attain other harmonic series. The player's right hand is inserted in the bell to make slight changes in pitch as well as quality. If the hand is cupped and nearly blocks the opening, the pitch is changed considerably and the tone muted. Incidentally, this right hand also holds the instrument in the correct position for playing.

The trombone is not unlike the trumpet or cornet except that instead of valves to add tube length, most are built with a sliding section of tubing, changing the shape of the instrument, which allows, incidentally, for an infinite number of harmonic series. Some trombones employ valves to change the tube length.

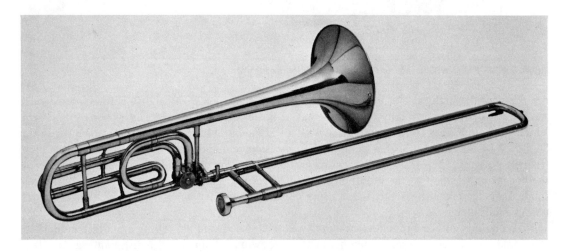

Figure 7.29.   Trombone (Courtesy of Conn, Artley, Scherl and Roth)

The tuba is the bass brass instrument. It is large and heavy. In order to carry the tuba on the march, John Philip Sousa invented a "sports model" which wraps around the performer so the weight rests on his shoulder, and is appropriately named the Sousaphone.

Figure 7.30.   Tuba (Courtesy of Conn, Artley, Scherl and Roth)

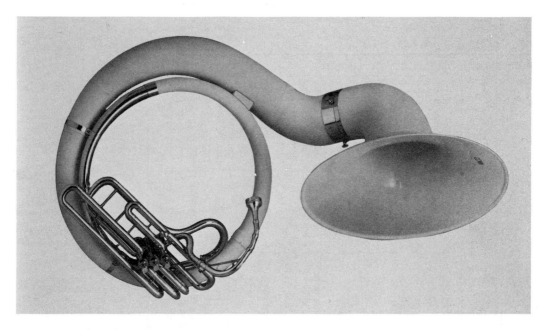

Figure 7.31.   Fiberglass sousaphone (Courtesy of Conn, Artley, Scherl and Roth)

Table 7-B

Brass Instruments

Name	Mouthpiece	Resonant Column	Concert (piano) Pitch Range	Transposing	Comments
Trumpet	Cupped	54″ (.35″ to .45″ dia., then flare to 4.5″)	E_3–Bb_5	Transposing (built in Bb, occasionally in F, Eb, C, & D).	First 5″ to 9″ of tubing is conical, then cylindrical to flared bell. Cornet has longer flared section with less cylindrical. Extra turn makes it appear shorter than trumpet. Tone similar, trumpet being somewhat more brilliant. Natural trumpets (fixed length) used before 18th century. Valves to alter length producing different harmonic series developed during early 19th century.
French Horn	Conical	148″, first ⅔ is conical, last third is exponential flare.	F_2–F_5	Built in F, occasionally in Bb and other keys.	Performer's right hand is cupped in bell to alter pitch and/or quality. Nearly complete closure mutes horn tone. Can overblow 16 partials.
Trombone	Cupped	Twice length of trumpet (108″), 0.5″ dia., cylindrical, then last ⅓ flares to 6″ or 8″ diameter.	E_2–Bb_4	Non-transposing although built in Bb. Also a tenor and bass trombone in F.	Developed in 15th century. Overblows 8 partials.
Tuba (Sousa-phone)	Cupped	Conical with flared bell pointing up, or horizontally	E_1–Bb_3	BBb most usual.	The Sousaphone (after John Phillip Sousa) might be called a sports-model Tuba which is easily supported on shoulder while marching.

Review Questions for Chapter 7. Wind Instruments

1. Be able to describe generally the evolution of wind instruments.

2. A tube, open at one end and closed at the other, will vibrate sympathetically to what partials? Which partials will be resonated by a tube open at both ends?

3. Be able to sketch the particle amplitude for the first three overtones in the closed and open tubes.

4. Which musical instruments operate as closed tubes? Which as open tubes? When a brass instrument (trumpet, trombone, etc.) overblows the partial series, does it sound both the even and odd partials? What about the clarinet?

5. How can one determine the length of an open tube to produce (resonate) a particular frequency? What about the closed tube?

6. What effect does the diameter of a tube have on its effective "sound" length?

7. What types of bores are usual for wind instruments? Be able to sketch each.

8. If you have two tubes of the same length, one open and the other closed, which will resonate the lower pitch?

9. If a wind instrument is tuned in a warm gymnasium, then taken onto the cold marching field, what will happen to the pitch? Why?

10. The sound source of wind instruments is produced in three different ways. What are they?

11. Of what material are reeds made?

12. Which instruments use single reeds and which double reeds?

13. How is the flute tone produced? What principle is employed?

14. Is a node or anti-node produced at the mouthpiece of the flute? Which is produced at the far open end? If the fundamental is played on a flute, is there a node developed within the tube? Where is it?

15. If a hole is opened on the side of a flute, what is the effective length of the tube? Is a node or anti-node produced at this opened hole?

16. What procedure can be employed to determine the efficiency of the air jet at the flute mouthpiece?

17. What anatomical parts are responsible for the shape of the air jet?

18. If the air jet spreads too much, how is the tone affected?

19. What causes a "goose note" or "squawk" on a clarinet? How should the clarinet reed vibrate?

20. Does the body of a flute, clarinet, oboe or bassoon vibrate appreciably? If it does not, does the material out of which it is made affect the tone quality?

21. Since the temperature of the air column within a wind instrument affects the sound velocity and thus the pitch produced, would a clarinet made of wood, or one made of metal, be affected more by changes in the ambient temperatures?

22. If a flute is overblown by increasing the jet velocity, would it be possible to play the pitches of bugle calls?

23. Be able to describe generally the evolution of brass instruments.

24. What is a natural trumpet? Is it very different from a bugle?

25. What do the valves on a trumpet do? There are two kinds of valves employed. What are they?

26. How does the interior shape of the brass instrument mouthpiece affect the tone quality?

27. Does a smooth and gradual bending of the trumpet tubing affect the pitch or the quality of the instrument?

28. How is it possible for a trumpet, or other brass instrument, to produce all of the pitches they play?

29. How many harmonic series does the slide trombone have?

30. How do the cornet and trumpet differ?

31. Since the metal of a brass instrument vibrates, does the metal thickness and mass affect the tone quality?

32. How do the tuba and Sousaphone differ? Why?

33. How are brass instruments muted?

CHAPTER **8**

The Pipe Organ

8.1 The Evolution of the Pipe Organ

Although some feel the pipe organ originated with the Syrinx (Pan Pipes), the earliest authentic records date back to c. 250 B.C. with the invention of the hydraulis by the Greek inventor, Ktesibios, of Alexandria. Wind pressure was provided by a water compressor rather than bellows. The hydraulis produced a loud, disagreeable tone which was more noise than music. It was used in Rome to accompany the gladiator fights and orgiastic rites.

A giant organ was built in the 10th century in England which required seventy men to operate the bellows supplying 400 pipes with air. Compare this with the largest organ in the world in the Convention Center at Atlantic City; it has 32,882 pipes, 1,233 stops, and seven manuals.

After 1300 A.D. the organ developed rapidly, one having 2500 pipes. Small organs were manufactured which were portable and carried in processions. In the 17th century, organs were built for which J.S. Bach wrote his music, and which serve as a model for the design of contemporary organs. The mechanics of the organ developed to a high degree and when electric power became available, electric motors provided the wind power. The organist's controls at the console operated electro-magnets which, among other things, controlled the "valves" for the air supply. Heretofore, a direct mechanical linkage from key to valve, called "tracker-action," controlled the air supply. Registration, the pre-setting of the stops chosen (a system of programming in modern vernacular), instantly made operational the ranks of pipes to be employed. Today, many organs again use the tracker-action.*

8.2 Construction of the Pipe Organ

The pipe organ is really a wind instrument which is operated by several keyboards (manuals). An additional set of "keys" (pedals) is operated by the feet. Normally each organ manual has 61 keys with a possible pitch range from C_o (16 Hz) requiring an open pipe about 32′ long, to C_7 (2048 Hz requiring an open pipe 3 1/3″ long).

---

*In about 1885, my father, then a young lad, had the job of pumping the church organ bellows. Occasionally, after a particularly long number, he tired, missing some strokes, resulting in a drop in air pressure and thus a decided sagging in pitch, much to the consternation of all concerned!

91

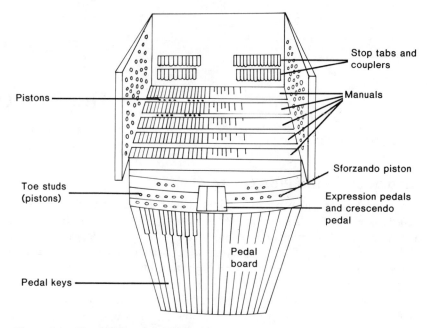

Figure 8.1.   The organ console (Artist: Colleen Rayburn)

Figure 8.2.   The pipe organ console. The five-manual Aeolian-Skinner organ in the Mormon Tabernacle, Salt Lake City, Utah. (Photo courtesy of The Church of Jesus Christ of Latter-Day Saints, Salt Lake City, Utah)

Figure 8.3. The organ console. The four-manual Moller pipe
organ in the National Shrine of Immaculate Conception,
Washington, D.C. (Photo courtesy of M.P. Moller, Inc.,
Hagerstown, Maryland)

8.3 Operation of the Organ Console

Manuals

The earlier instruments, called tracker organs, employed a mechanical system of levers and
wires to open the valves manually, allowing the air to pass through the pipes. On most contemporary organs, depressing a key makes an electrical contact that opens the valves magnetically.

There are from one to seven manuals (keyboards) with 61 keys each; the usual organ has
three manuals called the Choir, Great and Swell, which are operated with the hands, and one
pedal board with 32 pedal (keys) operated with the feet.

Stops

The organist determines which rank of pipes will sound by depressing the stop tabs, or
couplers which connect additional ranks of pipes.

Pistons

Once the organist has selected the ranks of pipes to be sounded, they can be pre-set to be depressed instantly with the pistons. Frequently the change must be made in a fraction of a second, so the pistons are indispensable. The pre-set combinations are called "generals." "Registration" is the pre-selection of the stops to be used. Other pistons, called toe studs, are operated with the feet.

Expression, Crescendo and Sforzando Pedals

The expression pedals open Venetian-blind-like shutters which separate the organ pipe chamber from the auditorium. Opening them allows the sound to pass through unobstructed so it increases in loudness from soft to loud. The crescendo pedal gradually adds stops (ranks) in discrete steps, also increasing the loudness by sounding more pipes. These are the only two ways to control loudness. The sforzando piston instantly brings the full organ into play.

8.4 Organ Pipes

Pipes vary in size and shape. They can be cylindrical, square, conical; they can be doubled back on themselves, hairpin style, if there is limited space. They can be made of wood, metal alloys (usually tin and lead—sometimes with zinc). It was believed that only wood and metal would make satisfactory pipes, but this belief has been dispelled; they could be made of cardboard, fibre glass, or any other practical, workable material. Unless the material is thin and flexible, it is principally the air cavity that counts.

The pipes can be open or closed. The closed pipe will sound an octave lower than an open pipe of the same length, but has a different quality since only the odd numbered partials are resonated.

The "pitch" of a rank of pipes, which is shown on the tabs, indicates the length in feet of the longest pipe in the rank—the lowest pitch. When C_4 (middle C) is played on a 32′ rank, the pitch heard is two octaves lower than C_4, or C_2; when played on the 8′ rank, it will sound the same pitch, C_4.

To strengthen a particular partial, a mutation stop is employed. For example, the Nazard 2 2/3′ strengthens the third partial; therefore it is never used alone. Other mutation stops are 1 3/5 and 1 1/3 feet.

A mixture is used in combination with other stops, consisting of two to seven ranks of pipes, to brighten the lower pitches.

There are two kinds of pipes: flue and reed. Flue pipes operate something like the flute in that an edge tone produces the sound. The most usual flue pipe is the diapason which is a cylindrical, open metal pipe. (Figure 8.4.)

A reed pipe (Figure 8.4) operates in principle much like the metal reed in a harmonica. Air flowing into the pipe causes the reed to vibrate. This reed can be tuned with the tuning wire which presses against the reed changing its vibrating length. The reed frequency must coincide with the fundamental frequency of its resonant pipe.

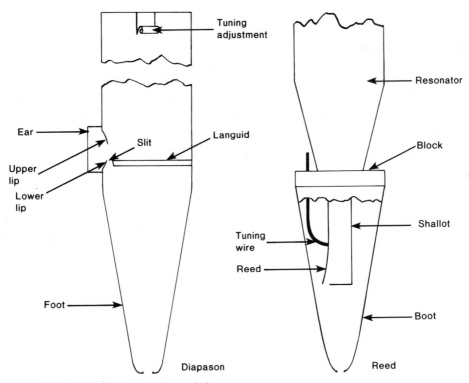

Figure 8.4.   The flue pipe and the reed pipe

8.5 Performing on the Organ

By now you can see that organists are very busy people. They must use and coordinate both hands and feet; read three staves (two for the hands, one for the feet); devise ways through registration to make certain tones louder without affecting the others because pressure on the keys ("touch") makes no difference in loudness as it does on the piano; move their fingers and feet in a smooth, connected manner since there is no sustaining pedal as there is on the piano; and manage to change the registrations and affect the other necessary controls of the instrument while they are performing.

8.6 The Electric Organ

Electric organs have been developed in which oscillators produce the pitches selected by the keys, and the waveshapes (sine, square, sawtooth, and others) determine the quality by judicious mixing and filtering the electrical signals developed.

The sound of the Hammond Organ is developed by tone wheels cut with a sine wave rippled edge, revolving in a magnetic field. This tone wheel increases and decreases the magnetic flux density which in turn develops a sine wave voltage. Each of the main tone wheels produces a partial, so the tone quality is determined by pulling out the stops (volume controls) for each partial. The relative intensities, of course, determine the quality. These partials are tempered whereas true partials are just intonation. The slight discrepancies in pitch seem to be unnoticed or easily tolerated by most listeners.

The Hammond has the advantage over many other electric organs in that it cannot get out of tune with itself. These tone wheels are geared together so they must rotate at exactly the correct speed with respect to the other tone wheels. Since a synchronous motor drives them, the pitch, like an electric clock, is as accurate as the frequency of your 60-cycle alternating current.

Review Questions for Chapter 8. The Pipe Organ

1. Be able to describe generally the evolution of the pipe organ.

2. Be able to describe the functions of the following parts of a pipe organ: stops, couplers, manuals, pistons, pedal keys, expression, and crescendo pedals. What does the sforzando piston do?

3. What two ways can the organist control the loudness of the pipe organ?

4. What is the length of the longest open pipe that can be used practically in the pipe organ? Why? What is the length of the shortest pipe?

5. What are the names of the two principal types of pipes in an organ? How do they work?

6. Explain generally how electric organs work.

CHAPTER 9

The Voice

The voice is sound uttered from the mouth of living creatures and used primarily as a means of communication. In humans it can be employed in singing as an artistic, acoustical means of expression in which, normally, pitches are sustained momentarily.

9.1 Forced Inhalation (Inspiration)

The lungs are made of highly elastic spongy tissue composed principally of air ducts and sacs. Air is drawn into the lungs through the mouth, trachea, bronchi and on to the alveoli by reducing the air pressure within the thorax below the atmospheric pressure. This is accomplished by muscular contraction to elevate the rib cage and pull the diaphragm down.

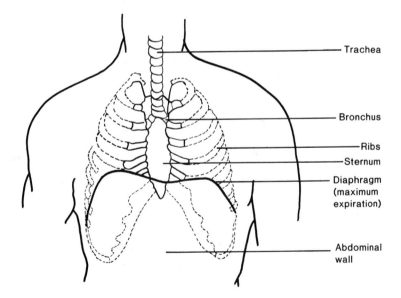

Figure 9.1. The breathing mechanism (Artist: Colleen Rayburn)

Having seen movies of Lilliputians who are one-twelfth our size, I speculated as to the pitch of their voice. If we make an appropriate change in length, tension and mass/unit length, a person who normally speaks at 220 Hz would increase in frequency to about 8,000 Hz. This would be a rather high, squeaky voice with only the first and second partials sounding in the audible range. This certainly would not be sufficient to communicate!

Each action increases the volume within the thoracic cavity and air enters through the trachea to equalize the pressure. However, when the diaphragm contracts, pulling itself down, it presses on the abdominal viscera which in turn distends the abdominal wall and pushes down on the pelvic cavity. When these muscles relax, the compressed structures mentioned return to their relaxed position.

9.2 Forced Exhalation (Expiration)

To expel the air, the abdominal wall contracts which compresses the viscera and forces the diaphragm up. Also, the rib cage is pulled down, thereby reducing the volume of the thoracic cavity. Note that muscles can contract or relax, but not expand themselves.

9.3 Lung Capacities

The volume of air within the thorax depends upon the size of the person. The values given in Fig. 9.2 are approximate, but provide an indication of the relative amounts.

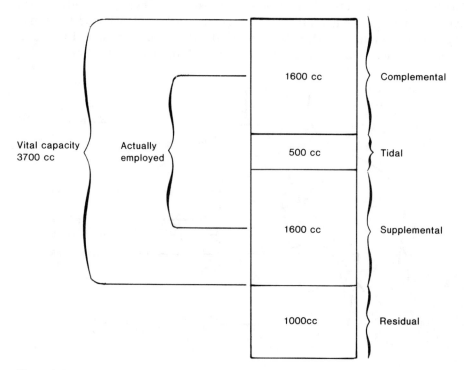

Figure 9.2. Average lung capacities

The vital capacity is the total amount of air which can be expired after maximum forced inspiration; the residual is that which remains after complete expiration and cannot be forced out. Tidal air is that which is used in normal, quiet breathing. The vital capacity is measured with a spirometer.

9.4 Vocal Sound Production

Air, expelled from the lungs, passes through the bronchial tubes and trachea to the larynx. The larynx (Adam's Apple) contains the vocal cords (vocal folds) which can be tightened and moved together. When air passes between the vocal folds (Figure 9.3), it sets them into vibration much as the lips of a brass player vibrate. The frequency of vibration is determined, as with a violin string, by the length, tension and mass. The male vocal folds are more massive and longer than the female's (male is 20 to 24 mm whereas the female is 14 to 17 mm long). This accounts for a difference in pitch of approximately one octave.

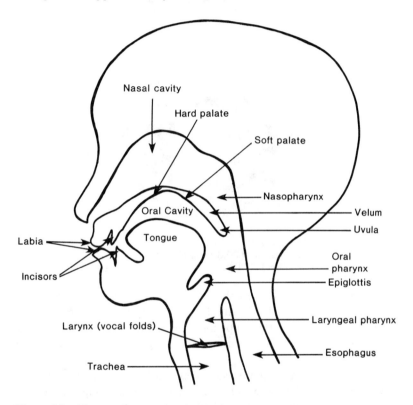

Figure 9.3. The vocal mechanism (Artist: Colleen Rayburn)

When the vocal folds vibrate, a series of puffs is emitted into the pharynx and then into the oral cavity. These puffs are not sinusoidal, therefore rich in harmonics. The resonators cause certain formants to be amplified which in turn change the vocal quality and permit verbal communication. The three principal resonators are the pharyngeal cavity (low frequency resonator of perhaps 190 to 300 Hz), the nasal cavity (mid-frequency resonator of around 580 Hz), and the oral cavity (high frequency resonator from 850 to 2560 Hz).

The basic determiner of tone quality is the pharynx. The soprano vocal process, for instance, has a smaller pharyngeal cavity than does the contralto whose voice is deep and heavy in quality. Although your parents determined the basic size of your pharynx, it is possible to alter its length somewhat by drawing the larynx down, thus lengthening the pharynx.

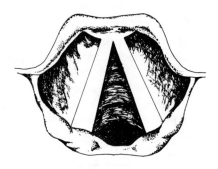

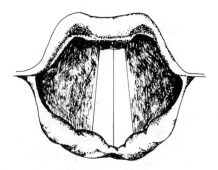

Figure 9.4. The larynx: During respiration (top); During phonation (bottom) (Artist: Colleen Rayburn)

The vowel qualities are determined by the oral cavity resonance controlled by the tongue and the labia. The vowels "ee," "ay" and "ah" are determined by the position of the tongue, whereas "oh" and "oo" require a change in the shape and size of the orifice by adjusting the position of the labia. (You can demonstrate this to yourself by saying "ah," "oh" and "oo" and noting the labial change.)

If the vocal folds do not draw together sufficiently, a breathy quality results. This is caused by "free" air passing between them which is not used in producing phonation. A whisper is produced in this manner and, being noise which is rich in high-frequency overtones, will be resonated by the oral, pharyngeal and nasal cavities so that effective communication can still be achieved without phonation.

Consonants may be defined as obstructed sounds (a complete or partial closure of the breath stream). They may be voiced (laryngeal vibration) or voiceless, consist of noise, may be explosive, and be expelled through the nose or through the mouth. The types of consonants are many and a detailed discussion is outside the scope of this study.

9.5 Vocal Classifications

The vocal types can be divided into the following six categories, three for women and three for men.

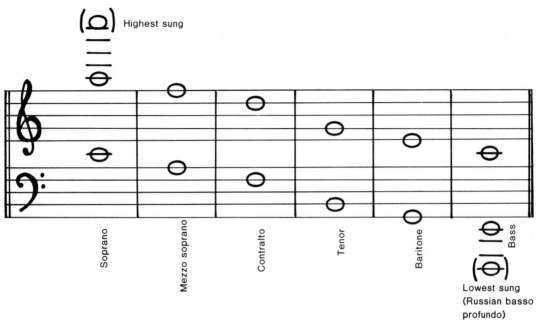

Figure 9.5.   Approximate vocal pitch ranges for untrained voices

Soprano: Highest pitched woman's voice, light in quality.
Mezzo-soprano: Medium pitched woman's voice, medium quality.
Contralto: Low pitched woman's voice, heavy quality

Tenor: Highest pitched man's voice, light in quality.
Baritone: Medium pitched man's voice, medium quality.
Bass: Low pitched man's voice, heavy quality.

Further classifications may be made as follows:

Dramatic: A powerful voice, appropriate in the more dramatic operas. Characterized by a rather pronounced intensity vibrato.
Coloratura: A voice capable of singing florid, colorful, ornate music.
Lyric: A light quality voice, characterized by a rather pronounced pitch vibrato.
Basso profundo: A man's voice, powerful and low pitch range, very heavy quality.
Cambiata: A boy's changing voice.
Castrato: A male soprano employing a falsetto or, during the 16th through the 18th century, the unchanged male voice retained by means of castration.
Treble: Higher pitched voices, female or unchanged boy's voices, and the countertenor.
Counter-tenor: A man's voice with a highly developed falsetto, the vocal equivalent of the castrato which is no longer used.
Falsetto: A high pitched vocal tone with a fairly pure harmonic structure such as that produced by the higher pitched tones of a yodel, due to the partial vibration of the vocal cords. The counter-tenor employs this type of tone production; the highest pitches produced by a woman are usually falsetto.

Review Questions for Chapter 9. The Voice

1. Be able to describe how forced inhalation and forced exhalation is accomplished.

2. Name, and be able to indicate the approximate volumes of air, as identified in this book. What instrument is employed to measure lung capacity?

3. Describe the process of phonation.

4. How do male and female vocal folds differ?

5. Do the vocal folds follow the same law as vibrating strings? What is this law?

6. Be able to sketch and identify by name and function the various anatomical parts involved in breathing and in vocal tone production and control.

7. Approximately, how much higher in pitch (or frequency) is the average female voice than the average male voice?   .

8. When the vocal folds phonate, how are "puffs" produced?

9. Is the tone produced at the larynx a pure tone, or rich in harmonics?

10. Name the three principal vocal resonating cavities. Describe the approximate frequency ranges for each of the three formants.

11. What is the name of the instrument used to examine the vocal folds? How would it be possible to examine the larynx during phonation?

12. What is the basic determiner of the vocal tone quality? What other controllable parts alter the vocal tone quality? What anatomical differences are there between producing "ah" and "oo"; between "ee" and "ah"?

13. What is the most probably cause of a "breathy" vocal tone?

14. Is phonation taking place when one whispers?

15. How is it possible to communicate when whispering since no phonation is occurring?

16. How are consonants defined?

17. How might one determine the lowest pitch to which the oral cavity will resonate?

18. Be able to describe the various vocal types as listed under "Vocal Classifications."

19. What are the approximate pitch ranges of the average, untrained singers?

CHAPTER **10**

Percussion Instruments

10.1 The Evolution of Percussion Instruments

The percussion family is considered to include the oldest form of musical instruments, appearing about 3000 B.C. This speculation is based on the designs found on cave walls and excavated crude pottery.

First, the primitives probably stamped on the ground, clapped their hands and beat their chests. Very early appeared percussive objects such as the rattle, strung with nut shells or teeth, tied with cords and hung from a stick, or tied to the ankles, knees, waist or neck of a dancer. Primitive people felt these rattles had magical powers which would frighten evil spirits.

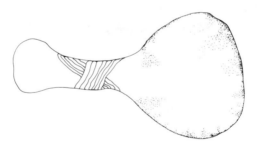

Figure 10.1. Gourd rattle (Artist: Colleen Rayburn)

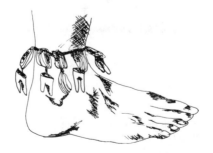

Figure 10.2. Rattle (tied to dancer's ankle)
(Artist: Colleen Rayburn)

This was probably followed by the stamper which consisted of a pit dug in the ground and covered with heavy, rough bark. One or two persons would dance on it, making a dull, hollow sound enhanced by the resonance of the pit.

Figure 10.3.   Stamper (Artist: Colleen Rayburn)

The slit-drum was made of a hollow tree trunk with a narrow longitudinal slit cut in its side. Men stamped on it and the resonance provided by the cavity improved the sound. Later, a small, easily portable slit drum was developed.

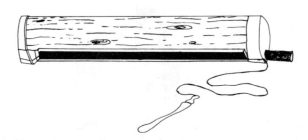

Figure 10.4.   Slip drum (top) and portable slit drum (with string) (Artist: Colleen Rayburn)

The early drum was made by stretching a membrane over a hollow body. It was struck with the bare hands, sticks or bones. An East African footed drum was made of a hollow log with three feet to support it on the ground. A membrane was stretched over the upper end to be beaten, usually with the hands. Other versions of the early drums were made from skulls or clay, and covered with a taut membrane. The two-headed drum evolved much later.

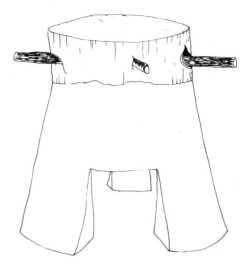

Figure 10.5. Footed drum (Artist: Colleen Rayburn)

Friction instruments also were used very early in history. A sound was produced by wetting the hand or applying a resinous substance to the fingers and rubbing the body of the instrument, a taut membrane or string attached to the instrument. This is similar to rubbing the top of a goblet with a wet finger. More recent, musical goblets, known as a "glass harmonica," were developed as a legitimate musical instrument by Benjamin Franklin, utilizing several rotating glasses. They were tuned by partially filling them with water. Among the composers using the glass harmonica were Mozart and Beethoven.

Figure 10.6. Glass harmonica (Artist: Colleen Rayburn)

About the same time as the evolution of the drum, scraped instruments were discovered. By notching a stick, bone, or shell-like body, and scraping it with a rigid object, a buzzing sound was produced. This type of instrument is still in use today.

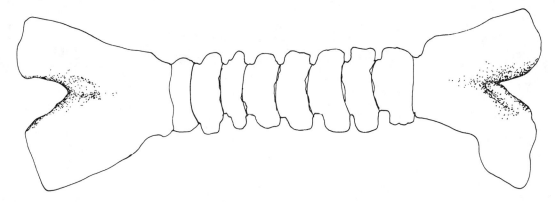

Figure 10.7. Scraped bone (Artist: Colleen Rayburn)

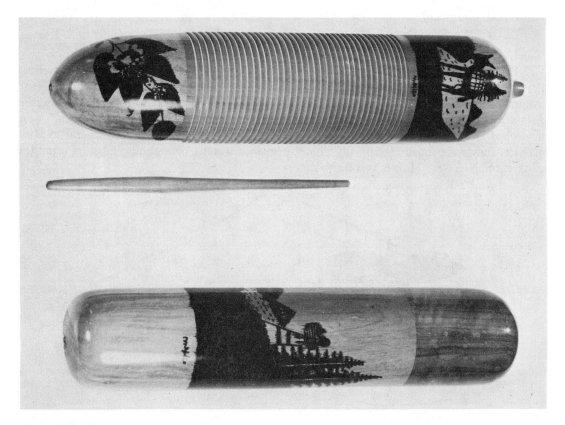

Figure 10.8. Modern gourd

Primitive man discovered that wooden bars, supported at nodal points, produced different pitches. These sticks originally were supported by the two outstretched, separated legs. From this crude instrument evolved the xylophone.

Figure 10.9. Primitive xylophone (Artist: Colleen Rayburn)

It will be quite evident, upon examining our contemporary percussion instruments, how most of them evolved. With the development of metals and plastics, many innovations have been made which provide us with a most exceptional and diversified family of instruments capable of providing most of the percussive-type sounds. The two principal types are the idiophones and membranophones. Idiophones are made of solid, resonant materials like the gong or marimba bar. Membranophones, as the name indicates, have taut membranes which are rubbed or struck as is the case with the drum.

Contemporary Percussion Instruments

A percussive tone is one which is produced by striking an object, followed immediately by a dying out, or decay, of the tone's intensity. Or the sound can be produced by scraping, which is unpitched noise such as that produced by sand blocks. The characteristics and operation of the various types of percussion instruments follow.

10.2 Membranophones

They include the kettledrums (timpani), tom-tom (snare drum), and bass drum. The membrane, made of thin animal skin (usually calf skin) or plastic, is stretched over a barrel-like resonator. The periphery is held fast so it always produces a nodal ring. These membranes are struck at any point on its surface, except the timpani which has a nodal point at its center, so that different overtones, and hence qualities, can be produced. One can consider the diameter of the head to vibrate like a string with nodal points at the ends. The fundamental frequency of a taut head is given by:

$$f = \frac{c}{D}\sqrt{\frac{T}{\sigma}}$$

where f = Hertz
     c = constant
     D = diameter of head
     T = tension
     σ = density of head/unit area

The above assumes the density of the head and the tension in all directions to be uniform—which is seldom, if ever, the case in practice.

There are two types of vibrational designs, nodal radii and nodal concentric circles. When the head is struck, it vibrates in all of its possible modes. Figure 10.10 shows some of the possible vibrational patterns with the lines representing the nodes.

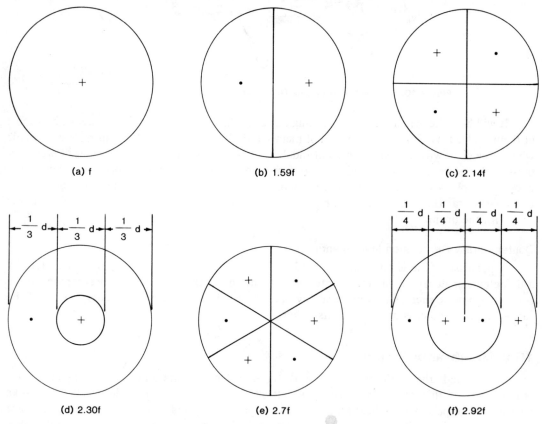

(a) f

(b) 1.59f

(c) 2.14f

(d) 2.30f

(e) 2.7f

(f) 2.92f

+ Motion down
• Motion up

Figure 10.10. Vibrational patterns of timpani head

10.3 Membranophones of Definite Pitch

Kettledrums (Timpani)

Figure 10.11.   The timpani family (Courtesy of Ludwig Industries)

The kettle supporting the timpani head is a parabolic or hemispherical bowl resonator. It is reasonably air-tight and reflects the sound energy. Most of the sound radiated by the timpani comes from the upper surface of the taut membrane. The "kettle" tends to encourage equal but opposite motion of the segments of the head, in a vibrational pattern inherent in a taut membrane. (When one sector moves down, increasing the air pressure within the "kettle" another sector moves up to equalize the pressure.) This probably accounts for the rather dead response when the timpani head is struck at its center causing the entire head to move down as a single unit. Normally, the timpani is struck at a point one-half the way between the rim and the center—an antinode.

10.4 Membranophones of Indefinite Pitch

Tom-Tom (Snare Drum)

The tom-tom and the bass drum usually have two parallel membranes covering the ends of a cylinder. When one head is struck, even at the center, the opposite head is depressed in the same direction a fraction of a second later, which tends to maintain a more constant pressure within the drum.

The snare drum is a tom-tom with snares (gut, plastic or metal helical springs) which rattle against the snare head when it vibrates. These snares produce a more crisp sound than without them. Usually, the snare drum is played with two wooden sticks which strike the batter head. The batter head is thicker and tougher than the snare head.

Bass Drum

The bass drum is a tom-tom type of drum but of greater diameter and depth, hence a lower pitched sound. It is played with one or two mallets, usually at or near the center of the head. It is used to punctuate music at the primary beats and to produce sound effects like the explosion of a cannon or the roll of thunder. The sound energy produced by the bass drum, because of the size of the head and its large amplitude of vibration, can be tremendous.

Other instruments within this classification are the tenor drum, the bongo and conga drums.

10.5 Idiophones of Definite Pitch: Tuning Fork, Orchestra Bells, Xylophone, Marimba, Bell Lyra, Vibraphone, Celesta, and Chimes

Idiophones are percussion instruments made of solid, elastic material such as metal or wood, which are struck, shaken, plucked, or rubbed. They may be tuned or untuned (definite or indefinite pitch).

Tuning Fork

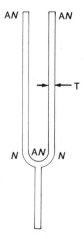

Figure 10.12.   Tuning fork

A simple tuning fork is not used in musical performance but provides a standard frequency or pitch. It is a bar, bent back on itself like a hair pin, with a handle welded to its center. The fundamental has two nodes and three antinodes. (Figure 10.12.) Antinodes are always located at the ends of the bar and at its center. When struck, the fundamental pitch and a high-pitched "clang tone" (about six times the frequency of the fundamental) are produced. The clang tone dies out rapidly leaving a nearly pure tone sounding. The frequency of the steel fork is nearly insensitive to temperature, varying 1 vibration in 10,000 per degree Centigrade. It is for this reason that they provide an excellent standard frequency. Although the frequency of a fork is determined empirically by the manufacturer it is roughly $f = \dfrac{k\,T}{L^2}$ where L = length, T = thickness in the direction of vibration.

Orchestra Bells (Glockenspiel), Xylophone, Marimba, Bell Lyra, Vibraphone and Celesta

All of these so-called keyboard instruments (because they are arranged like the keyboard of a piano) employ vibrating bars as the sound source. These bars are supported at nodal points. For the fundamental pitch, the antinodes are located at each end with nodes 0.224L from the ends. (Figure 10.13.) These bars are struck at the middle or ends (antinodes) of the bars with mallets which may be hard, or covered with felt or rubber to "soften" the tone quality.

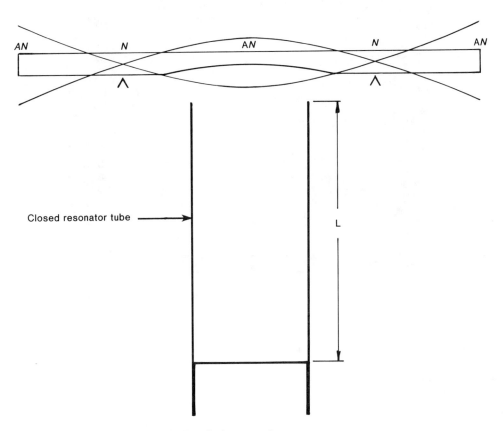

Figure 10.13. Marimba bar with closed tube resonator

The bars are tuned by adjusting their length and thickness. The frequency is dependent upon the mass and stiffness of the bar material, and the length. Since the thickness of the bar in part determines its stiffness, thinning it at the center where there is the maximum amount of bending will reduce the stiffness causing it to vibrate with a lower frequency. Shortening the bar, of course, will increase the frequency.

The Celesta

The celesta resembles a small upright piano and is played with a piano-like keyboard causing hammers to strike steel bars. It plays harmonic as well as melodic passages.

Figure 10.14.   The celesta. Note the keyboard, tuned bars and resonators.

Chimes

Chimes, or tubular bells, consist of a set of metal tubes, suspended from a frame, and tuned chromatically to piano pitches. They are struck at the top end (antinode) and suspended a few inches from the top end (node) with cord or raw hide. They produce an abundance of inharmonic overtones which may be accentuated or suppressed by crimping the tubing to encourage the development of nodal points.*

---

*The world is full of interesting sounds, many of which are too faint to be heard. To illustrate one example, tie a piece of store string to the handle of a table fork, allowing the ends to extend perhaps two feet. Holding the ends of the strings over the thumbs, press the strings firmly against the ears, closing them. Allow the fork to swing, striking a solid object like a table. You will hear a chime! If the string is touched to the needle of a phonograph pickup, this sound may be amplified many times, with a very striking effect.

10.6 Idiophones of Indefinite Pitch: Cymbals, Triangle, Tambourine, Traps

Cymbals

Cymbals are made from hard brass employing a "spinning" process, similar to spun aluminum pans, which forms the proper shape and further hardens the metal. An examination of a cymbal will reveal the spiral indentations made by the spinning tool.

The cymbal, like the bell, has a node at its center and nodal rings and radii over its surface, much like the patterns of the timpani heads except the cymbal locates its maximum antinodes at the periphery. Since a node exists at the center, a handle or leather strap may be attached at that point to hold the cymbal for performance.

The cymbals are struck together with a slicing action, necessary to avoid the production of a vacuum, or with mallets. The hard mallets emphasize high frequency overtones, whereas a felt-covered or rubber mallet emphasizes the low-frequency overtones, giving a more mellow quality. They can be struck together to give a crash emphasizing a particular beat, or struck in a lighter manner joining the bass drum to give a pulse. A single, suspended cymbal can be struck or rolled upon to give emphasis, create excitement or anticipation, or make an ethereal sound.

Triangle

This instrument is a steel rod, bent into the shape of a triangle. Incomplete closure of this triangle leaves the ends free to vibrate as antinodes. It is supported at one of of the closed vertices of the triangle (nodal points), and struck with a metal rod, or rolled to produce delicate effects. The sound is very high pitched and penetrating; the inharmonic overtones are clearly perceptible.

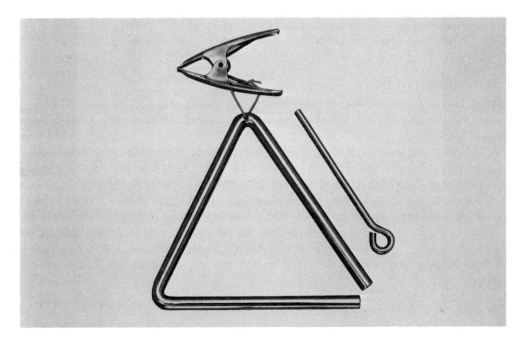

Figure 10.15.   Triangle (Courtesy of Ludwig Industries)

Tambourine

This "gypsy" instrument has a single head, mounted on a shallow cylinder in which there are holes for the insertion of "jingles" or small metal discs. It is struck with the hand or with a moistened finger skipping on the head to produce a continuous tone. The tambourine can be shaken to produce a rattling-jingling effect. It is used frequently in Spanish or Gypsy music.

Traps

Figure 10.16.   Traps

There are countless other traps used for particular sound effects such as the anvil, castanets, maracas, thunder machines, wind machines, bird whistles, boat whistles.

10.7 Evolution of Bells

With the coming of the Bronze Age, man experimented with objects made of the alloy of copper and tin, discovering that the sound made by striking it was interesting. From these initial experiments came today's bells.

The oriental bell was barrel-shaped, providing a variety of overtones. The Romans used the Tintinnabulum (latin for "tinkling") as signals long before they had any musical application. Before castings were available, a bell was made by hammering a sheet of bronze into a square, cutting out the corners, then bending the sides together, fastening the joints with rivets. This "cow bell," which produced a rather unmusical rattle, was brought to Ireland c. 450 A.D. by Roman missionaries. Since there was no tin in Ireland, the bells were made of iron, a poor substitute. Early cup bells were made also of porcelain and earthenwear. The earliest bells had thick walls, a convex exterior shaped like a beehive, and were struck on the outside with a hammer.

Figure 10.17.   Early "cow bell" (Artist: Colleen Rayburn)

Figure 10.18.   Beehive bell (Artist: Colleen Rayburn)

Hand bells, a small type, c. 1100 A.D., were hung, and struck with a hammer. When the series had four bells, it was called a "quadrillionem" which in French is "carillon." More bells were added until twelve or fifteen hung in a series. Manuscripts and carvings on cathedral walls in France fix the date in the 12th century. These bells were tuned to scale pitches, with one or several being played simultaneously.

Near the end of the 15th century bells were rung by a clock. The mechanism operated much like the escape mechanism in a clock with a revolving cog-wheel activating the tones. The use of bells in churches dates back to the 6th century on the continent and the 10th century in England. The exterior shape of the bell ceased to be convex and became more conical or concave at the beginning of the 13th century.

A bell may be rung in three ways: chiming, when the bell is moved allowing the clapper to strike it; ringing, when the bell is rotated in a full circle, providing a very intense tone; clocking, in which the bell is held motionless and the clapper pulled to strike it. This latter method very often cracked the bell.

A peal is the successive ringing of tuned bells. The English and American peal bells have a major third instead of a minor third overtone which prevents them from being played together due to the unpleasant resultant tones.

The "perfect" bell has the following significant overtones which are harmonious when played together. For comparison, the overtones of the English pealing bell are provided.

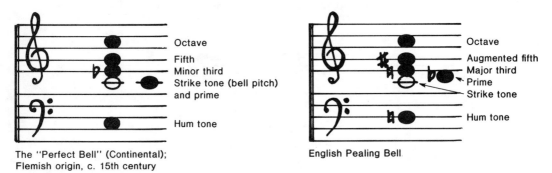

The "Perfect Bell" (Continental);
Flemish origin, c. 15th century

Figure 10.19. Bell overtones

The harmonic series has a major third interval with the strike tone pitch, not a minor third. The minor third gives the bell its characteristic quality. The continental bell's overtones are so perfect that when played together, a most pleasing effect is produced. This was not true with the English bell until fairly recently. If the waist of the bell is too thin, the pitch of the fifth is flat; the strike tone depends on the thickness of the lip.

Riverside Church in New York City, has a bourdon bell weighing 40,926 pounds, and a diameter of 10.2 feet. The largest bell ever cast was the Tsar Kolokol of the Kremlin in Moscow, 1734, and destroyed by fire in 1737. It weighed c. 500,000 pounds with a diameter of over 20 feet. The largest bell in existence today is the Trotzkol in Moscow, weighing c. 350,000 pounds. The pitch of a bell varies inversely with the cube root of its weight.

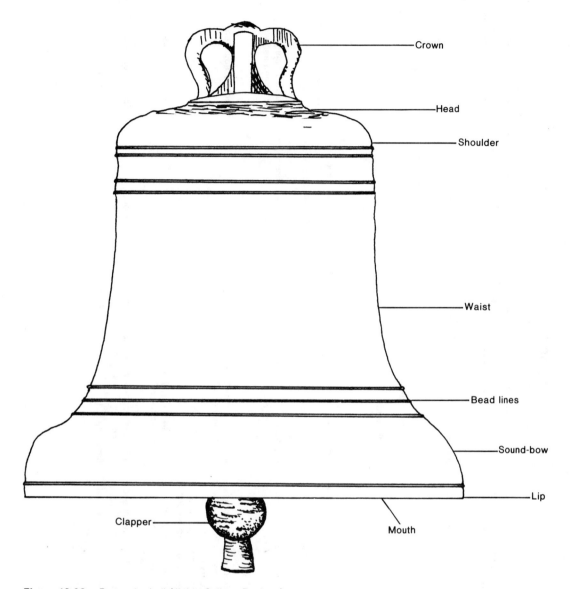

Figure 10.20.   Parts of a bell (Artist: Colleen Rayburn)

Table 10-A
Percussion Instruments

Instrument	Vibrating Material	Pitches	Decay Rate	Resonators	Tuning Procedure
Membranophones of Definite pitch					
Timpani (Kettledrum)	One head of animal skin or plastic.	23″ diameter D_3–A_3 26″ diameter $B\flat_2$–F 28″ or 29″ diameter F_2–C_3 32″ diameter D_2–A_2	Long	Parabolic bowls	Increase tension of head with hand screws or foot operated cables.
Membranophones of Indefinite pitch.					
Tom-tom (snare drum)	Two heads (sometimes only one) of animal skin or plastic.	Indefinite	Very short	Concert drum: short cylinder Street drum: long cylinder	Tension adjusted with key.
Bass drum	Two heads of animal skin or plastic.	Indefinite	Medium	Large cylinder	Tension adjusted with hand screws.
Idiophones of Indefinite pitch.					
Cymbals	Work-hardened brass concave discs. (Beryllium or phosphorus alloyed with brass to harden.)	Indefinite (many inharmonic overtones heard).	Long	None	Factory adjusted
Triangle	Metal rod bent into shape of triangle, ends unjoined.	Indefinite (many inharmonic overtones heard).	Medium	None	Factory adjusted
Tam Tam (Gong)	Work-hardened brass alloy	Indefinite (many inharmonic overtones)	Long	None	Factory adjusted
Tambourine	Single head of animal skin or plastic stretched over shallow cylinder which holds small metal "jingle" discs.	Indefinite	Short	None	Untuned

Idiophones of Definite pitch.

Instrument	Construction	Pitch range	Duration	Resonators	Tuning
Chimes (tubular bells)	Metal tubes suspended vertically, struck on end with wooden mallets.	Tuned chromatically from C_5–F_6	Long	None	Factory tuned to tempered scale.
Glockenspiel (orchestra bells)	Steel bars	G_3–C_6	Medium	None	Factory tuned to tempered scale.
Xylophone	Wooden bars	F_3–C_7	Very short without resonators; medium with resonators.	None, usually	Factory tuned to tempered scale.
Marimba	Wooden bars (recently fiberglass reinforced epoxy resin).	A_2–C_7	Medium	Closed tubes to resonate odd numbered partials	Factory tuned to tempered scale.
Bell Lyra	Cast aluminum bars	A_4–A_6	Medium	None	Factory tuned to tempered scale.
Vibraphone	Cast aluminum bars	F_3–F_6	Short or long depending on resonators	Closed tubes with rotating butterfly discs.	Factory tuned to tempered scale.
Celesta	Steel bars struck by hammers, actuated with piano-type keyboard.	C_3–C_7	Medium	None	Factory tuned to tempered scale.
Bells	Bronze (copper & tin) and cast iron	Strike tone pitch variable	Long	None	Factory tuned

Review Questions for Chapter 10. Percussion Instruments

1. Be able to describe generally the evolution of percussion instruments.

2. What is the definition of a percussion instrument tone?

3. What are membranophones and idiophones?

4. Of what materials are the various percussion instruments made?

5. How is the frequency of vibration of a membranophone related to diameter, tension, and the density of the head per unit area? Is this similar to the law of vibrating strings?

6. What nodal configurations are found in membranophones and idiophones?

7. Where is the timpani head struck? The bass drum?

8. Which membranophones are "definite pitch" and which are "indefinite pitch"?

9. Be able to describe the shape and other significant characteristics of the Orchestra Bells (Glockenspiel), Xylophone, Marimba, Bell Lyra, Vibraphone and Celesta.

10. Where are the vibrating bars, as on the marimba, supported? Where are they struck?

11. Which of the idiophones are of definite pitch? Which are indefinite pitch?

12. Which of the idiophones produce principally harmonic overtones? Which principally inharmonic overtones?

13. What is a "glass harmonica"? Who invented it? Have they ever been used in serious symphonic music?

14. For what two purposes are hollow tubes placed beneath some of the idiophone bars? Are these open or closed tubes? How do they affect the tone quality?

15. Describe the material and construction of cymbals.

16. What are the phase relationships between adjacent vibrating sectors of a membranophone or cymbal? Be able to draw the nodal configurations for each.

17. What is the principal difference in the overtones produced when striking a cymbal with a metal or hard mallet, and with a soft or rubber mallet?

18. How are idiophone bars tuned?

19. Do chimes produce harmonic or inharmonic overtones? How can certain harmonics be enhanced or suppressed by the manufacturer? Where are chimes struck?

20. Be able to describe some of the "traps."

21. How did the bell evolve? About when did bells first appear? What bell, still used today, was probably the first made?

22. Which bells, Continental or English, can be played together satisfactorily? Why is this true? What are the pitches and names of the principal overtones?

23. What is the largest bourdon bell every cast? How much did it weigh? Where was it cast? Where is the largest bourdon in the United States, and what does it weigh?

CHAPTER 11

Electronic Music

For hundred of years, many thousands of people have been composing music, and evolutionary changes have been evident and necessary as the possible melodies, harmonies, rhythms, tonalities and timbres became exhausted. Add to it the boredom that developed as people tired of the old and longed for something new and different. We have already witnessed, among other changes, the increased use of dissonance, polytonality or the abandonment of tonality, and the increasing complexity of rhythm, to mention a few. These changes parallel the other arts—painting, sculpturing, architecture, literature—because of a need to explore the new and the unknown. Electronic music is a natural step in this evolutionary process, wedding sound with the exploding electronic technology.

For many, some kinds of electronic music are not music at all, but rather "interesting sounds." This, of course, depends on one's definition of music. But such changes will occur, and should occur, with science and technology having an ever increasing effect on the art of musical sounds. It is interesting to speculate as to what tomorrow will bring.

Early (1945–1965), electronic music usually referred to live sounds, and electronically or mechanically contrived sounds which have been stored on magnetic tape to be manipulated, synthesized, organized, and perhaps re-recorded for a taped performance. Today, the definition has been broadened to include live performance with electronic instruments, synthesizers, the electric guitar, electric organs and others. For those who have not heard an electronic music concert, it will be a unique experience when the stage curtains part, revealing only a tape recorder, amplifier and two or more banks of loud speakers. Perhaps a soloist, or several, will appear to play with the taped sounds.

11.1 Sound Sources

Some of the raw material from which sounds in electronic music are derived are electronic oscillators (sine, square, sawtooth, pulse, triangular)* and others with a frequency range over the audible spectrum. Other electronic devices produce white or dark (pink) noise. The computer is another source for sounds with the potential of almost unlimited manipulation. Live (concrète) sounds, subsequently manipulated, are derived from the human voice or any other sound-producing object.

---

*Formulas may be found in the Appendix.

11.2 Sound Modifiers

Any device employed to control sound is called a sound modifier. Following are examples: (1) oscillators and other sound generators, (2) amplifiers, (3) fixed variable audio filters to allow the selection of certain portions of the audio spectrum, (4) multi-track tape decks capable of recording sound-with-sound or sound-on-sound to synchronize and mix other sound material, (5) envelope generators to control the amplitude of a given sound, (6) ring modulators and harmonic frequency shifters serving as a frequency multiplier, altering the characteristics of sound material in countless ways, (7) mixers to combine separate signals into one or more channels, (8) a keyboard serving as a preprogramed device to control oscillators and other electronic units, (9) reiteration employing multi recording-playback heads to cause a gradually fading restatement of material, (10) electronically contrived reverberation, usually employing a helical spring or an extremely thin steel plate where the sound is applied to the metal, then picked up some distance away; acoustical reverberation employing an echo chamber (hard surfaced room) in which the sound emanates from a loud speaker and is re-recorded with a microphone located in the chamber some distance away.

11.3 Time Modifiers

It may be desirable to control the various tonal parameters with respect to time. This is accomplished with variable speed tape decks with information changers which permit tape information to change pitch or speed without affecting the other parameters; by sequencing program signals in different time relationships. Other controls appear as the art and science of electronic music matures.

It is interesting and exciting to witness this musical-scientific evolution in the search for new means of musical expression.

Review Questions for Chapter 11. Electronic Music

1. What are some of the reasons that prompted the development of electronic music? About when did this occur?

2. Describe how electronic music is "composed."

3. From what sources are the sounds derived? What are concrète sounds?

4. What is meant by "sound modifier"? What specific ways do sound modifiers control the sounds?

5. What is a time modifier? How is this accomplished?

CHAPTER 12

The Hearing Process

12.1 The Structure of the Hearing Process

Sound enters the ear by way of a tube (auditory canal) which is terminated by the eardrum (tympanum). (Fig. 12.1.) On the other side of the tympanum is an air-filled cavity—the middle ear—which is connected to the oral cavity by means of a tube (Eustachian tube), which serves to equalize the pressure between the middle ear and the atmosphere.

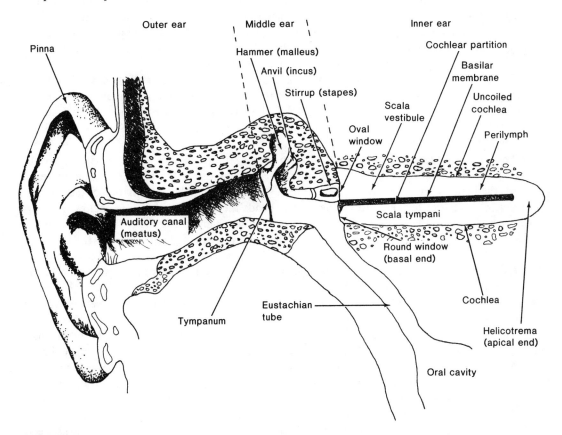

Figure 12.1. The hearing mechanism (Artist: Colleen Rayburn)

Within the inner ear are three small, connected bones (the ossicles) which serve to conduct the sound from the tympanum to the inner ear. They are named the hammer (malleus), anvil (incus), and stirrup (stapes). The stapes is connected to the oval window (a membrane which closes off one end of the liquid-filled spiral-shaped tube known as the cochlea in which the hearing nerves are located). (Cochlea is a Latin word meaning "snail.") The other end of the cochlea is terminated with another membrane known as the round window which opens into the middle ear and allows for the motion of the liquid (virtually non-compressible) when the oval window is depressed by the stapes.

12.2 The Dynamics of Hearing

When sound enters the auditory canal, it causes the tympanum to vibrate back and forth, moving the ossicles as a lever mechanism, which in turn moves the oval window. The oval window acts like a piston transmitting the vibrations to the liquid within the cochlea which in turn brings about an activation of the cilia and the auditory nerves. The displacement of the ear drum is very small, being 0.00000001 cm or 10^{-8}cm for ordinary conversations. Compare this to a cigarette paper which is .0036 cm thick. The ossicle mechanism of the middle ear mechanically amplifies by its lever system the pressure applied to the oval window by a factor of approximately 2. The ratio of areas of the tympanum and the oval window is between 15 and 30. This means that a total mechanical amplification of the ossicles is from 30 to 60 times.

The cochlea is a spiral-shaped cavity in the bony structure of the skull. It has 2 3/4 turns, is about 1 1/3″ long and about 1/8″ in diameter at its widest point and is divided over nearly its entire length by a partition. On one side is the Scala Tympani and on the other, the Scala Vestibuli, both filled with a liquid. The oval window (at the basal end) opens into the Scala Vestibuli; the round window terminates the scala tympani.

The cilia (hair-like structures) extend from the organ of Corti. When a pressure wave depresses the oval window, the cochlear partition must give—first at the basal end, then traveling towards the helicotrema which it reaches in about 0.003 seconds. The deformation of the cochlear partition with respect to the tectorial membrane bends the cilia. This bending excites the nerve endings producing in the brain the sensation of sound. Just where, along the cochlea the excitation takes place is a function of the frequency, with the highest frequency registering at the basal end and decreasing in frequency towards the apical end (at the Helicotrema). The different frequencies excite different nerves and therefore different places in the brain. This gave rise to the "place theory of hearing" since it is the place that is activated which determines the pitch. Partial destruction of the nerves within the cochlea raises the hearing threshold at the "place" destruction occurred.

The place theory does not explain the hearing of subjective tones since we hear a pitch whose nerves are not excited. There are other phenomena which cannot be explained by the place theory.

After an auditory nerve is fired, about 1/300 second is required for it to recharge for refiring. This means that no single nerve can fire more than about 300 times per second requiring nerves to fire successively, the order depending upon their respective levels of sensitivity. This successive or alternate discharge of the nerves in bursts is called the Volley Theory of Hearing.

Synchronized volleys occur below about 1000 Hz. Above this frequency the discharges seem to occur in rather random order. This would suggest that the place theory would explain the ability to discriminate in pitch at high frequency, whereas the volley theory would explain this phenomenon at lower frequencies. I studied many musicians to determine how high in frequency a tone could be and still retain its pitch identifying characteristics. None of those studied was able to identify the pitch by letter name for tones whose frequencies exceeded 8,000 Hz, even though we can hear tones over an octave higher.

It is fairly well substantiated that loudness perception is due to the number of nerves firing per second since when a nerve fires, it gives up its entire electrical charge—not just a part of it. It should be kept in mind that a complex tone consists of a number of pure tones (partials or overtones) so the total intensity results from the summation of the partial intensities.

It is not possible, with our present knowledge, to provide a definite explanation of the auditory functions. Experimental work continues in an attempt to sift the myriad of findings by countless investigators to explain the hearing process.

12.3 Subjective or Aural Harmonics

Real or objective harmonics which are tones produced outside the ear have already been discussed. There is another harmonic or tone which is generated in the hearing mechanism and heard by the brain but does not actually enter the ear. They are called subjective or aural harmonics.

The hearing mechanism is a non-linear receiver in that the displacement is not directly proportional to the force. This means that a pure tone of sinusoidal shape will be distorted by the hearing mechanism with one-half of the wave developing a greater force than the other half. This distorted force means that harmonics have been added (changing its shape) with an accompanying change in quality. The degree of distortion is a function of the intensity so the weak sinusoidal tone will sound quite "pure," but as the intensity is increased, the waveshape distortion increases rapidly. This distortion takes place even though the waveshape of the tone entering the ear remains sinusoidal. A good example of distortion due to excessive loudness is when you increase the volume of your radio until the amplifier and speaker are being overdriven and the tone quality is impaired.

12.4 Measurement of Hearing: The Audiogram

A sinewave oscillator may be employed to determine an individual's auditory threshold, represented by a curve which indicates the minimum intensity perceptible over the audio frequency range. The oscillator is adjusted to various frequencies with the volume control turned down to zero. Then, gradually, the intensity is increased until the subject indicates that he can just hear the tone. Several measurements are made at each frequency employed. This process is repeated at various frequencies until enough values have been obtained to plot the audio threshold curve. (Fig. 12.2.) The instrument employed by an audiologist to measure hearing acuity is called an audiometer.

Sound intensity is measured in the watts of power impinging on one square centimeter of surface. An automatic lathe becomes annoying at .000001 watts; a battery of cannons, .001 watts. An increase of ten billion times over the faintest audible sound (at the auditory threshold) becomes painful physically. Keep this in mind for future reference when the subject of sound pollution is discussed.

When measuring the hearing response, acoustical intensity may be measures of voltage, or the amplitude of a sine wave, or a volume control which has been calibrated.

If, at any frequency setting, the intensity is increased until the maximum loudness is reached—that is, any further increase in intensity will not produce an increase in loudness since all the auditory nerves are firing—the intensity value of the pain threshold has been attained. It is fairly well established that an eight-hour exposure to sound at an 85 dB level, will permanently damage the hearing mechanism.

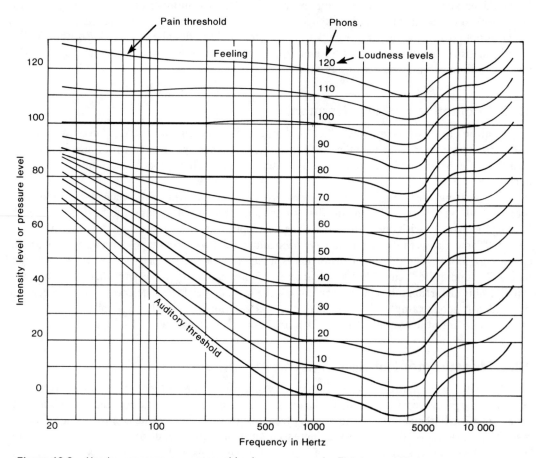

Figure 12.2.   Hearing response curves: equal loudness contours by Fletcher and Munson.

12.5 Decibels

The unit of power ratio was named after Alexander Graham Bell and is called a Bel. This unit is so large, however, that the decibel or dB (1/10 of a Bel) is the one in common usage. It is the ratio of two values of electrical or acoustical power equal to ten times the common logarithm of the ratio.

$$dB = 10 \log \left(\frac{P}{P_0}\right) \text{ which is equal to } 20 \log \left(\frac{E}{E_0}\right) = 20 \log \left(\frac{I}{I_0}\right) \text{ where } P = \text{intensity}$$

or power, E = voltage and I = current.*

As an example, if a one volt signal is applied to an amplifier and a 100 volt signal is obtained at the output (a voltage gain of 100), $dB = 20 \log \frac{100}{1} = 20 \log 100 = 20 \ (2.0) = 40$ dB gain.

In acoustical research the reference level of 0 dB = 10^{-16} watts per cm² which is equal to 0.0002 dynes per cm². This is the threshold of audibility for a 1000 Hz pure tone, the standard reference frequency.

12.6 The Phon

Since the loudness of a tone is a function of frequency, the constant-loudness contours were obtained by comparing the loudness of sounds at various frequencies with that of a standard pure tone of 1000 Hz. For instance, to obtain the loudness contour for 40 phons, the first point plotted would be 40 dB above the threshold of audibility at 1000 Hz. Then a second point, perhaps at 200 Hz, could be plotted by adjusting a 200 Hz tone to have the same loudness as the standard 1000 Hz tone, giving the second point (dB value) on the 40 phon contour. This process may be repeated for different dB levels of the 1000 Hz tone to obtain a family of contours, known as the Fletcher-Munson curves, presented in Fig. 12.2. Incidentally, an increase of 10 dB doubles the loudness of a tone. Doubling the power produces an increase of 3 dB. The minimum perceptible difference (mpd) in loudness a person can detect is approximately 1 dB.

12.7 Binaural and Stereophonic Sound

In this age of stereo reproduction it might prove interesting to know just how directional sound works.

Stereophonic sound is based on loudness. In other words, if a person standing to your right speaks, the sound entering your right ear will be louder so you know where he is. Therefore, when a stereophonic recording is made of a symphony orchestra, microphones are placed all around the stage to pick up the different instrumental groups. The signals from each microphone are fed to the recording engineer who can mix them (with the aid of a trained musician) and record them on the left or right channels with the proper balance. A mixer is required for each microphone input. It is interesting to note that the engineer can switch the stage position of a group of instruments from one side of the stage to the other by merely "flipping a switch." In the theaters the sound comes from the right and left stage, or right and left walls of the auditorium, and gives the impression of direction.

If sound source location were based on loudness, partially closing one ear would change the direction of the sound source. This does not happen.

Binaural sound means hearing with two ears and the directional effect is based largely on phase. If a sound is directly in front or in back of you, or any place in the sagittal plane, it is not possible for a person with his eyes closed to locate the sound source because the sound arrives at

*A Table of Logarithms may be found in the Appendix.

the two ears at exactly the same time. If, however, the sound source is to one side of the sagittal plane, the sound will arrive at one ear a fraction of a second before it arrives at the other ear, because of different distances it must travel, and the brain can differentiate between the times of reception. Because of previous experience of coordinating sound and sight, it is possible to assign quite accurately the direction of the sound source.

Perhaps you have noticed that a dog, on hearing a strange sound, cocks his head to the right, then left, trying to locate the sound. Undoubtedly he is trying to get the sound source out of the sagittal plane. We, too, if hearing a sound while lying down, will sit up and cock our head to locate the sound source, just like the dog.

An interesting experiment to try is to have a friend close his eyes, then you click two coins in front of him, above him, or in back of him—always clicking in the sagittal plane. When asked to point to the coins when clicked, he will seldom locate the direction correctly. If he does, it is by accident.

It is interesting to note that two oscillators adjusted to say 500 and 501 Hz, one being fed into the right earphone and the other into the left earphone, will produce the effect of a single sound revolving about the head once a second. This is due, of course, to the fact that the tones are in-and-out of phase once each second.

Sound source location is not possible with monaural hearing unless reflections from the walls or some other clue are provided. It is for this reason that a very deaf person, hearing with one ear (the hearing aid), cannot locate the sound source. If he were to employ two complete hearing aid systems, sound source location would be possible.

When you are seated at the banquet table in a very noisy room, it is possible for you to focus your attention on one conversation across from you, not hearing what others are saying, then make a mental shift and concentrate on another conversation, not hearing the first. This is because of binaural hearing and your ability to focus your attention in a particular direction. The hard-of-hearing individual, relying on a monaural hearing aid, cannot do this since he does not have the directional sense. For this reason the deaf person frequently becomes distressed when there are confusing sounds within the room such as loud conversations, the television or radio blaring, since he cannot concentrate on a conversation. Remember this and be understanding of their problem.

12.8 Masking

A loud sound can drown out, or mask, a weak sound because the auditory nerves being used by a loud sound are not available for the weaker. A very loud tone can mask tones of higher, but not lower frequency, probably because of the harmonics of the loud tone, whether they be real or aural harmonics developed within the hearing mechanism.

An interesting experiment you might like to try is to negate the effect of masking by noise while trying to telephone in a very noisy room. Most of us cover the ear not being used by the telephone, but that is not the ear masking the conversation. Instead, cover the telephone mouthpiece so that the masking sounds do not enter the ear receiving the conversation. I understand that telephones have been tried which have a button switch on them to cut off the microphone signal and thus avoid the masking effect. Unfortunately, this scheme was not practical because the user would forget to release the button when he wanted to talk!

It is not very encouraging for an orchestral performer to discover that his instrument is masked by the loud brass section so he might just as well stop playing.

12.9 Pitch and Frequency Discrimination

Since early in this century one of the psychological studies of considerable interest to music educators has been the measurement of pitch discrimination—the ability of a person to detect minute difference in pitch. Carl Seashore, of the University of Iowa, was a pioneer in the field of the Psychology of Music and studied this area. He developed a series of recordings which could be used by educators to measure this capacity which he considered a music aptitude with predictive value. His findings indicated that the best human ears could detect a difference between 500 and 501 Hz, one vibration per second difference. Some years later in my own laboratory, due to greatly improved electronic instrumentation, I found the best ears could discriminate a difference in pitch between 440.0 and 440.1 Hz. (A very accurate way to measure the differences between two tones of nearly the same frequency is to employ beats or Lissajous figures. With the aid of a stop watch, differences of less than 0.1 Hz can be measured.) But another type of discrimination came to light—frequency discrimination. Pitch discrimination demands that a difference in the highness or lowness of a tone be perceived. When the differences in frequency become small enough, the subject is unable to effect a pitch judgement but knows the tones are not the same. Finally, the difference in frequency may be decreased sufficiently that the subjects can hear no difference between them and indicate that they are the same, even though they are not. This identifies another discrimination level, frequency discrimination, where pitch is not involved.

I studied many so-called monotones, the "tin ears," and found that the poorest score was made by an individual who had a pitch discrimination level of about 1.0 Hz at A = 440 Hz. When one considers that the difference between A and $A^\#$ is approximately 26 Hz, this "tin ear" had the ability to discriminate much more accurately than necessary to sing and hear in tune. I worked with many "tin ears" and in a very short time had them all singing quite well in tune, certainly well enough to continue improving on their own. The inability to sing in tune is not related to the hearing mechanism, but rather it is a kinesthetic problem, a problem of affecting proper laryngeal adjustments, a problem of muscular control.

12.10 Absolute and Relative Pitch

A person who can name a pitch, without reference to one that is known, is said to have absolute or "perfect" pitch.* If the subject has heard an identified reference pitch and then can identify other pitches, he is said to have relative pitch.

Having absolute pitch can be a great help, such as pitching a song or tuning an instrument. For some it is bothersome because when a musical selection they know is written in a certain key, but is being played in another key, it sounds wrong. Or, if the speed of their phonograph is slightly off, they sense the discrepancy which bothers them.

---

*At the National Music Camp (Interlochen, Michigan), many of the campers, all accomplished musicians, claimed they had absolute pitch and were escorted by their friends to my laboratory to find out if it was true. There was so much interest and competition in this area that a "Keen Ear Club" was established and a weekly group test given. Those who could identify 19 out of 20 randomly sounded tones on the Bell Lyra were given a special membership certificate! To see if this ability could be trained, I played a tone on the piano at each meeting of my college conducting class. The students tried to identify the pitch, wrote it on a piece of paper, and signed it. After turning in their papers the pitch was replayed and identified. Records were kept of their responses to check their improvement—if any. They were asked to try to sing a pitch whenever they passed a piano, then play it to check themselves. Before the semester was over almost the entire class of 40 students was able to identify the pitches.

Review Questions for Chapter 12. The Hearing Process

1. Be able to sketch the outer, middle and inner ear. Label each part, including the eustachian tube and the oral cavity, and be able to identify the function of each.

2. Distinguish between the "place" and "volley" theories of hearing.

3. After a nerve is discharged, approximately how long does it take to recharge and be ready to "fire" again? If this is the case, what is the maximum frequency to which a single nerve can respond?

4. Where does hearing take place? In the ear, or the brain?

5. What causes the cilia to move? What happens when they move?

6. How is the degree of loudness explained by the hearing theory?

7. When an auditory nerve "fires," does it produce an electrical potential (voltage) proportional to the amount of physical deformation the cilium has experienced?

8. What is a subjective harmonic? An aural harmonic? How do they differ from real harmonics or objective harmonics?

9. What is the name of a graph which indicates the sensitivity of the hearing mechanism over the audible range? Give the name of the curve representing the minimum intensity that can be heard. Give the name of the curve representing the maximum loudness over the audio frequency range.

10. What is a decibel? A phon? How are they related? At what frequencies is the ear the most sensitive to sound?

11. How does the intensity of a sound vary with the distance between the source and the listener?

12. What is "masking" and how is it accomplished?

13. When telephoning in a noisy room, how can your hearing a conversation be improved? Why does this happen?

14. Describe the differences between binaural and stereophonic sound. On what does each depend to give direction to the sound source?

15. What will be heard if a 500 Hz pure tone is fed into the left ear, and a 501 Hz tone is fed into the right ear? Explain why this happens.

16. Why does a very deaf person wearing a hearing aid have difficulty understanding a conversation in a noisy room? How might this situation be corrected?

17. What does the term "sagittal plane" mean?

18. How accurately can some people sense a difference in the frequency of two tones at the 440 Hz level?

19. What is the most accurate way to measure minute differences in frequency when studying the sensitivity of the hearing mechanism?

20. Is there such a thing as a "tin ear"? Where does the difficulty lie if not in the hearing mechanism?

21. An increase of how many decibels doubles the loudness of a tone?

22. Define binaural and stereophonic sound. How do they differ? Can binaural sound be listened to with loud speakers? What about stereophonic sound?

CHAPTER 13

The Vibrato: Musical Ornamentation

The vibrato is a musical ornament which, to some, improves the tone. It is a periodic change in pitch (frequency modulated), loudness (amplitude modulated), timbre (harmonic modulated), or a combination of these, occurring at a rate of nearly seven per second. Carl Seashore, a pioneer in the study of the Psychology of Music, studied the vibrati of 29 singers and found that the mean rate was 6.6 per second (from 5.9 to 7.8) and the mean extent was 0.48 of a tone (from 0.31 to 0.98). The vocal intensity vibrato gave a mean rate of 6.27 per second, with an average extent of 3.3 dB.

A change in pitch requires a laryngeal change, therefore the pitch vibrato must involve a laryngeal tremor; a change in intensity requires a variation in air flow, therefore it probably involves a diaphragmatic tremor; a change in timbre requires a change in the resonant cavities (oral, pharyngeal, nasal, lip orifice), so the tremor must originate with one or more of these parts. Often, one can observe the tremor below the chin (tongue) of the singer, and when the mouth is wide open, pulsations of the tongue, velum, and even the jaw itself.

Most instrumental performers employ a vibrato which is produced in many different ways. They may employ the types of tremor mentioned, or it may be a rapid voluntary movement of the jaw, or moving their fingers on their instrument (trumpet). The trombone occasionally moves the slide slightly which would suggest a pitch vibrato. Actually, the trombone slide vibrato is an intensity vibrato, usually not believed by the trombonist until shown, probably because the instrument shakes against the embouchure negating any change of pitch made with the slide and leaves only a change in the loudness of the tone. Some instruments, such as the clarinet, do not use a vibrato except in "popular" groups. It is interesting to note the change in the acceptance of vocalists without a vibrato. Many of our contemporary "Rock" or "Folk" groups have singers without previous vocal training, so a perfectly smooth, unornamented tone for these vocal groups is now considered the most desirable.

Sometimes the term tremolo is used in place of vibrato. To most musicians, the vocal tremolo is an undesirable, uncontrolled, excessive type of vibrato. The vibrato effect on a pipe organ, however, is called a tremolo. In this case, it is a variation in intensity, or loudness.

One of my graduate students, working for her master's degree in speech, studied the vibrato in the speaking voice and found it is employed to heighten the dramatic-emotional effect of speech.

At the National Music Camp, while studying the vibrato of a professional cellist, I found in a lyric passage she produced a pitch vibrato by moving her finger rapidly against the string, rolling the fleshy pad at the finger's tip. Then she demonstrated she had another type of vibrato which she used in dramatic passages. This we studied and found it to be almost entirely an intensity vibrato. She attained this by grasping the instrument firmly, compressing the pad, so that her vibrato movements literally shook the cello. This intrigued me so I studied the vibrato characteristics of lyric and dramatic singers and found the lyric to possess predominantly a pitch vibrato whereas the dramatic had predominantly an intensity vibrato. Without too much effort I was able to eliminate the laryngeal tremor (which obviously produces the pitch vibrato) of some students and replace it with a diaphragmatic tremor (which produces the intensity vibrato) changing their vocal classification from lyric to dramatic voices. The pedagogical application of these findings is valuable indeed for the voice teacher.

Review Questions for Chapter 13. The Vibrato: Musical Ornamentation

1. Be able to define "vibrato."

2. What is the approximate mean vibrato rate?

3. How is a vibrato produced on various instruments, including the voice.

4. Is a vibrato desirable? When is a vibrato not employed?

5. Be able to describe the various ways in which a vocal vibrato is produced.

6. Does a vibrato have any effect on vocal type identification?

CHAPTER **14**

Recording

14.1 Disc Recording

In 1877 Thomas Edison made the first recording on a wax cylinder by affixing a diaphragm to the end of a horn (megaphone) which had a cutting stylus mounted at its center. As the diaphragm moved, the stylus moved up and down cutting a "hill-and-dale" sound track of varying depths. To hear what was recorded the process was reversed—the stylus was allowed to ride in the groove causing it to move up-and-down, moving the diaphragm which in turn created the sound.

Next, a spiral groove was cut in the surface of a wax disc with the sound moving the stylus laterally to cut a wiggly groove reproducing the waveshape of the sound (as it would be seen on the oscilloscope). In the early days, the actual cutting and reproducing was done with acoustical power; later electromagnets were modulated with an amplified sound. As the current increased, the magnet became stronger; as it decreased, the magnet became weaker with an appropriate movement of the cutting needle. To play the recordings a transducer (device for changing mechanical energy to electrical energy, or vice versa) developed a feeble voltage proportional to the displacement of the needle. This voltage was then amplified many times until sufficient to drive a loud speaker (also a transducer).

Various methods were tried to record two audio signals for stereophonic recordings. The one used presently records one signal on one side of the groove and the other signal on the other side. (Fig. 14.1.) Transducers are mounted at right angles to one another (45° to the surface of the disc) so that motion from one side of the groove will move the transducer perpendicular to its surface; and the other side of the groove, the other transducer. This provides two separate electrical signals which can be amplified separately and heard over different loud speakers.

14.2 Tape Recording

Magnetic tape is a ribbon of plastic on one side of which is painted, presently, a coating of iron oxide or chromium dioxide. As this tape is drawn across the gap of an electromagnet driven by an audio amplifier, the magnetic field across the gap, varying with the signal, will magnetize the iron oxide. (Figure 14.2.) If, then, the tape is drawn across the gap again, this time with the head feeding into an amplifier rather than out of it, the variations in magnetic strength will develop a changing magnetic flux in the iron core and thereby develop a voltage in the wire winding—just like a transformer. This feeble voltage may then be amplified to drive loud speakers.

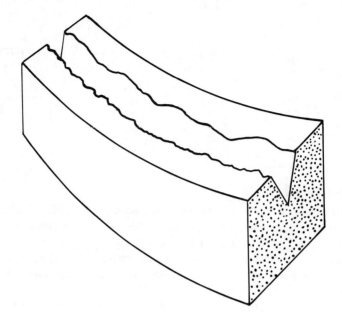

Figure 14.1A.   Stereophonic recording groove.

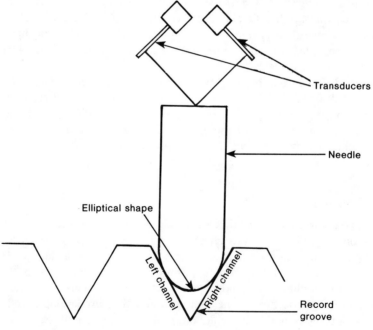

Figure 14.1B.   Stereo pickup

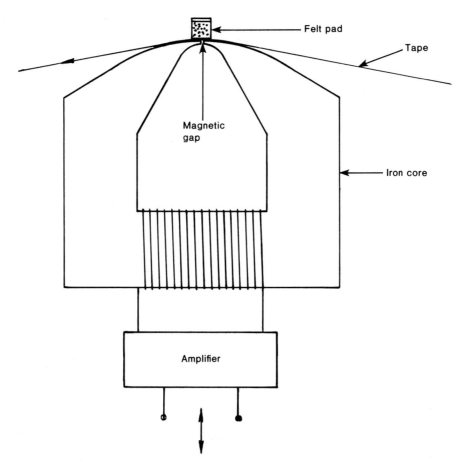

Figure 14.2. Tape recording and playback head

The highest frequency that can be recorded depends principally upon the tape speed and the width of the magnetic gap. If the tape runs too slowly, or the gap is too wide, one cycle will be recorded on top of the previous cycle impairing the quality of the recording. Tape speeds are usually 15, 7 1/2, 3 3/4 and 1 7/8 inches per second.

If the tape is recorded at too high a level, the iron oxide will saturate magnetically and flatten the peaks of the sound waves. This, of course, produces distortion. The maximum intensity range presently possible is an amplitude ratio of about 100:1 (40 db). If the tape is highly magnetized, and the plastic strip very thin, one loop on the reel will magnetize the tape lying in contact above and below it (print through). This will give a pre and post echo effect.

Four track stereo recordings are made by recording (Figure 56) two signals on two separate tracks (A and B). Playing in the reverse direction they would be recorded on C and D. Since the total width of the tape is 1/4″, each signal has but 1/16″ recording width. (Fig. 14.3.)

Magnetic tape usually is erased by recording an ultra-sonic sine wave tone over the previous signal which it obliterates.

Figure 14.3. Four-track tape

14.3 Sound on Film*

The sound track will be found along the edge of the motion picture film. There are two types of sound track—variable width and variable density. In both cases the amount of light that can pass through the film is caused to vary because of the width or density of the black silver deposit. Note the picture of a variable width track, Fig. 14.4. The transmitted light falls on a photo cell which in turn develops a voltage proportional to the amount of light it received. This varying voltage is then amplified to drive the loud speakers.

Recently a strip of magnetic oxide has been placed along the edge of the film for audio recording.

It should be noted that although the picture frames move through the projector in jumps, the sound track portion, off-set from the pictures, obviously must move past the photo cell with absolutely constant velocity. Also, the light which passes through the sound track must be of constant intensity.

---

*The first person to put sound on film, in July of 1922, was Professor Joseph Tykociner, a young Polish-American engineer in the Department of Electrical Engineering, University of Illinois. One day, when he was reminiscing about his earlier years, he told me the story about his first sound-on-film which he so graciously played for me. He had recorded his wife saying, "See the pretty bell, hear the pretty bell." Then, she rang a little bell several times. The sound was amazingly good. When he turned the material over to the university so they could obtain a patent, they sought the advice of a very well known man in the photography business who said there was no future in the idea so the patent was not secured. Another company, however, followed through on it and even today, "Hollywood" must pay this company for every foot of sound film they produce.

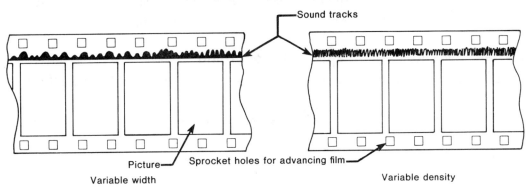

Figure 14.4. Optical sound tracks on motion picture film

14.4 Microphone and Speaker Placement for Stereo

Microphone and speaker placement is pretty much a trial-and-error process, but you might consider this as a starter.

Let us assume you are going to record a symphony orchestra or a play on stage. A minimum of two directional microphones is required. (Omnidirectional microphones which are equally sensitive in all directions clearly will not work.) One set-up would be to place the microphones close together well above the floor level, at center stage about 20′ into the audience and aimed out at about 30° to 45° from the mid-line. This will cause them to act like your two ears and differences in both loudness and phase will be recorded. The second method would be to use many directional microphones, four to eight hung above the stage to record all essential areas. Those on the right side would feed into one channel, those on the left side into the other channel. They should be fed through two mixers so an appropriate balance can be attained between microphone signals. The recording engineer, monitoring the signals, can effect a proper balance.

To play a stereo recording, the speakers normally should be mounted on the narrow wall off the floor to avoid having the sound blocked by people or furniture, and in from the corners about 1/4 to 1/3 the width of the room. Naturally, the best listening position will be near the center-line (equi-distant from each speaker) and not too near the speakers to avoid a silent center zone, nor too far from the speakers lest the stereo effect disappear. In the event the speakers must be widely separated, as at the sides of an auditorium stage, it might be well to introduce another mixer-amplifier-speaker system, fed by both signals and located at center stage midway between the two side speakers. This will feed both signals out of the center and fill the void.

How large an amplifier do you need? A 20-watt amplifier can blast most wives out of the house, but an amplifier-speaker system that will handle considerably more power should be used, employing only a fraction of its power capabilities so as to minimize distortion. Also, you will need a speaker system that reproduces, with an appropriate contour, all of the frequencies recorded. This probably means woofers, mid-range speakers and tweeters, mounted in a carefully designed cabinet, or poly-planar speakers which provide fairly uniform response over the frequency range. The frequency response of your speaker system is dependent to a great extent on the size, shape and design of your speaker cabinets.

Review Questions for Chapter 14. Recording

1. Disc recordings have been cut with two different types of impressions. What are they?

2. What is a transducer? What transducer is employed in disc recording or reproduction?

3. How is it possible to record two audio signals (two microphones) on one disc groove?

4. With what type of coating is a plastic tape covered to permit an audio signal impression?

5. What are the usual tape speeds for home recorders?

6. What is the relationship of tape speed and magnetic gap width to the frequency response?

7. With the presently developed tapes, what dynamic range in decibels may be expected?

8. Be able to indicate where, on a quarter-inch tape, four microphone signals are recorded, as for stereophonic recording.

9. How is a tape recording erased?

10. Describe how an optical sound track operates.

11. What non-optical sound track is now being used with some motion pictures?

12. Where are microphones placed when recording stereophonic sound of an orchestra?

13. Where are the microphones placed when recording binaural sound of an orchestra?

14. Where should speaker systems be placed to reproduce stereophonic sound in a living room?

CHAPTER 15

Architectural Acoustics

Perhaps it is unfortunate that architectural acoustics, at the moment, is not an exact science, but a combination of science and art. There are many calculated guesses still required, based upon experience and trial-and-error, when designing a building for optimum sound characteristics. However, the following material is presented to assist in avoiding many of the usual problems encountered.

The material in this chapter is presented in an elaborative outline form, for the check-list approach seems to be the most usable yet still supplying the explanations and procedures necessary in a step-by-step solution to the acoustical problems.

15.1 Site Survey
A. Sound levels.
    1. Definition of decibel (First presented in Chapter 12. Please refer to page 130).
    2. Typical sound levels.

Table 15-A
Sound Levels

Power Ratio	Loudness Increase	dB	Sound Source
10^{12}	× 4096	120	Threshold of feeling, jet take-off Nearby thunder, artillery, siren or riveter Boiler factory, construction jack or pneumatic hammer Rock band
10^{10}	× 1024	100	Power mower, heavy traffic, symphony orchestra playing full volume Unmuffled truck, noisy factory, police whistle (Permanent damage to hearing if above 85 db)
10^{8}	× 256	80	Noisy office, congested city traffic, loud party Average radio or factory, average street noise Typical kitchen
10^{6}	× 64	60	Noisy home, average office, ordinary conversation at 3′ Suburban street, quiet radio
10^{4}	× 16	40	Quiet home or private office Quiet conversation Rustling leaves
10^{2}	× 4	20	Quiet evening outdoors Quiet whisper at 5′
		0	Threshold of audibility

(For every 10db increase, the loudness is doubled.)

Acoustical intensity in watts per unit area decreases with the square of the distance. Therefore, the loudness of the above sounds is dependent upon the distance from the sound source and the listener, "D."

$$I = \frac{1}{4 \pi D^2}$$

B. Location and orientation of building relative to ambient sounds.
   1. Check with City Planning Commission regarding proposed changes. Develop and enforce Noise Abatement regulations.
   2. Sound intensity decreases with the square of the distance. The inverse square law:
      $$I = I_o/d^2$$
      where I_o = sound intensity of the source.
      I = sound intensity at listener.
      d = distance from sound source to the listener.

   3. Usual disturbing noise sources: traffic (trains, trucks, motorcycles and cars with defective exhaust systems), aircraft, construction (jack hammers, riveting, machinery), congregation of people (children's playground, athletic events, musical organizations), nearby industrial noise.
C. Reflection of sound from large, flat surfaces (buildings, walls).
D. Location of "quiet areas" above or below the street level. Note the cosine law:

   $$I = I_o \cos \theta = I_o \frac{d}{z}$$
   where I = intensity of sound impinging on building at target.
   I_o = Sound intensity at ground level.
   d = Perpendicular distance from sound source to building.
   z = Diagonal distance to target.

E. Landscaping. Trees, bushes and grass absorb sound as well as dust from gravel roads. The building should fit into area décor and architectural style.
F. Measurement of ambient sound levels. Employing an accurate decibel meter, using the dbA scale which represents the hearing sensitivity over a wide frequency range, measure the sound levels around the proposed foundation throughout the day and evening, and over a week's interval. These measurements will help determine the orientation of the building and the design of the exterior shell.
G. Decisions required:
   1. What changes in ambient conditions are predicted?
   2. What sound level can be tolerated within each part of the building? With appropriate funds, any building can be made absolutely quiet inside, but this may be too expensive. Occasionally, standards are specified, as in U.S. Government buildings.
   3. For greatest economy, the "quiet areas" should not face noise sources, and should be subterranean or located on the upper floors.

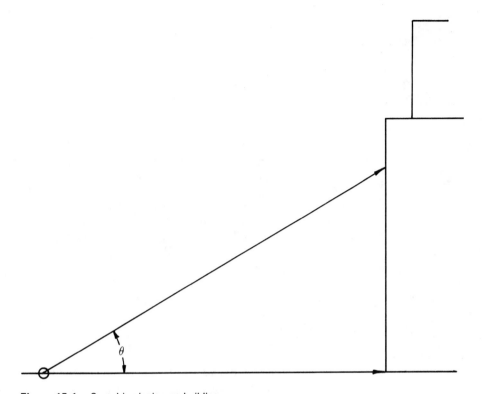

Figure 15.1.   Sound impinging on building

15.2 Sound Isolation: Airborne Sounds

A. Shell construction

Employ a massive shell. A sealed cement block wall attenuates the sound by 45 to 50 db. Doubling the weight of a wall increases the attenuation by only 5 db; therefore double, isolated walls should be employed.

B. Wall construction

Materials should be as massive as practical. The two surfaces should be mechanically isolated, employing staggered studs or other scheme. Drywalls, or plaster, mounted on studs, allow for the transmission of sound through the stud to be radiated from the second surface. An air gap between the wall surfaces reduces the conduction of sound to a minimum. Filling the spaces between the wall surfaces with insulating material such as fiberglass does little to reduce the sound transmission. It will, however, eliminate the fire "chimney," reduce heat transmission, and will eliminate the cavity acoustical resonance.

Walls and doors should be sealed so no leaks are present. A hole, $1'' \times 1''$, will reduce the sound attentuation of a wall from 50 down to 40 decibels.

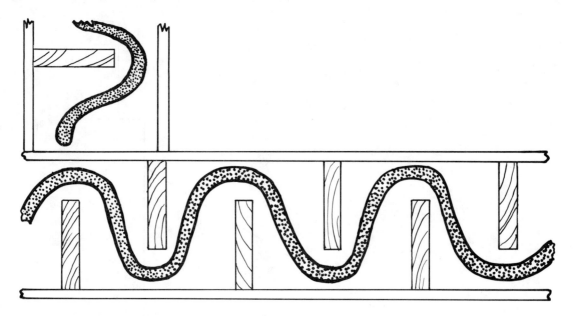

Figure 15.2. Staggered stud construction with fiberglass bats

C. Floor-ceiling-wall junctions

The floor to ceiling-below construction needs careful consideration to eliminate the transmission of sound from the floor above, such as footsteps. Carpet the floor and shock mount the floor joists or mechanically separate the floor from the ceiling below. A suspended ceiling may be employed. Care must be taken to seal the tops of the walls.

D. Window construction

Where sound and/or heat are important considerations, double glaze or thermopane construction is recommended. Two 1/8″ panes, separated 6″ to 8″, will provide a 40 db attenuation. The panes must be shock mounted and sealed to prevent moisture condensation and dust contamination. A 1/4″ plate glass is better due to the increased mass. Large panes will be resonant to low frequencies. The cavity between the panes will also be resonant but to a much higher frequency. To prevent cavity resonance, the panes should be mounted non-parallel, preventing a sharp resonance at a single frequency.

E. Door construction

For adequate acoustical isolation, doors must be as massive as possible and present no sound leaks. To prevent intermittent passage of sound, two doors with a vestibule (sound lock) between, or revolving doors may be used. Two 2″ solid wood doors, well sealed, forming a "sound lock," will provide a 45 db attenuation. (A hollow core door, not sealed, provides but 15 db attenuation). Quite effective hollow core doors are available, made with two separated shock-mounted panels. If they have small windows, double separated panes should be used.

Another reasonably effective "door" is the labyrinth hallway, with all surfaces lined with absorbent material.

F. Ventilators

Open grills, obviously, should be avoided if sound isolation is desired. Since most buildings today have central heating and air conditioning, highly absorbent (fiberglass-type) linings should be employed near the openings into the various rooms. This is especially important when confidentiality is required.

G. Baffles

To attenuate sound within the room itself, reasonably massive baffles (partial room dividers) or those constructed with mechanically isolated surfaces may be employed. Huygens' principle shows that sound will go around a corner, but the intensity is considerably reduced to tolerable levels. Reflected sound over the baffles can be reduced to a minimum by employing highly absorbent ceiling tile, rugs or carpets, and perhaps wall absorption, adjacent to the baffles.

H. Fans and blowers.

Employ large diameter fans, rotating at a slow speed, to reduce the nosie. Also, use lined ducts where necessary.

I. For confidentiality, use white noise or music on the innercommunications system. This will mask conversations preventing the listening to/or recording of a speech.

15.3 Solidborne Sound

A. Impact sound

Hammer blows or footsteps are best eliminated by reducing the impact sound with cushioning such as carpets, foam insulation or springs. Another way is to mechanically isolate the involved surfaces, thereby eliminating most of the airborne sound, as well as the direct conduction of sound through the solid materials. Many attempts have been made to eliminate impact sound by applying acoustical tile to the ceiling. Although acoustical tile absorbs reflected sound, it has but little effect on transmitted sound.

B. Machinery

Employ machinery which is well designed and constructed so there is no unnecessary built-in sound source, such as is produced by eccentricity. Isolate machinery to a place remote from the acoustically quiet areas. Machinery may be shock mounted on rubber, even sections of tires, fiberglass batts, pneumatic devices, or springs. Springs will absorb the low, but not the high frequency vibrations.

C. Structural supports

Solid members will conduct sound throughout a building. Prevent the vibrations from getting to the member. If necessary, members can be shock mounted on springs, rubber or fiberglass batts. Commercially available material will help you solve this problem.

D. Plumbing sounds

Employ quiet equipment. Insert in the water pipes a syphon or section of high pressure hose to eliminate much of the sound conduction. Liquid will still conduct some sound. An air chamber will help absorb the "steam hammer" impact.

15.4 Sound Reflection within a Room

A. Echo, the intelligible reflection of sound

   1. Velocity of sound, $V = 1054 + 1.1\, T°_F$, where V is in feet per second, T in degrees Fahrenheit.

   Refer to the graph relating temperature and sound velocity, Fig. 1.4.

   Echo becomes noticeable and objectionable when the reflecting surface is 50′ or more causing approximately 0.09 second delay. Therefore large, hard, flat surfaces such as plaster, cement block, plaster or wood panel walls at the end of a large room (over 50′ in length) should be avoided.

   2. Elimination of echo may be accomplished by absorbing the sound on the reflecting surface, or diffusing the reflected sound with convex surfaces, or angled wall surfaces.

B. Flutter echo

   1. Flutter echo is a rapid, staccato-like, multiple reflection of sound between two parallel, reflecting surfaces (walls) separated by less than about 20′.

   2. Flutter echo may be avoided by absorbing the sound on one or both of the two parallel walls, or by making the walls non-parallel to eliminate sharp resonance.

C. Ripple echo

   1. Ripple echo is the multiple, successive echo effect as produced from the seat risers in a stadium, each reflection delayed an additional fraction of a second due to the uniform increase in distance.

15.5 Reverberation

Reverberation is the multiple reflection of sound, heard as a gradually decaying sound as in a gymnasium. This is due to the sound being reflected and re-reflected from many hard surfaces within a room. Too much reverberation creates a background of sound that interferes with music and especially with speech. Some reverberation is desirable, but an optimum amount should be sought. Following is the method for calculating the approximate reverberation time, T.

$$T = .05 \left(\frac{V}{\Sigma\, a_n \beta_n} \right)$$ where T is the time in seconds for the sound to die out to one-millionth (60db) of its initial intensity (power); V is the volume in cubic feet; a_n is the surface area in square feet; β_n is the coefficient of absorption (percent absorption) of the surface for a given frequency, often at 500 Hz. A table of absorption coefficients will be found at the end of this chapter.

15.6 A Hypothetical Problem

Specify the acoustical characteristics for an auditorium to be used principally for speech, given the dimensions 60′ wide, 100′ long and 40′ high. The basic construction of the floor and ceiling are to be made of concrete, the walls of concrete block. The audience capacity is to be 750 maximum, with an anticipated average of 500. The speaker area across the north end of the room is 15′ deep. Following are the necessary calculations.

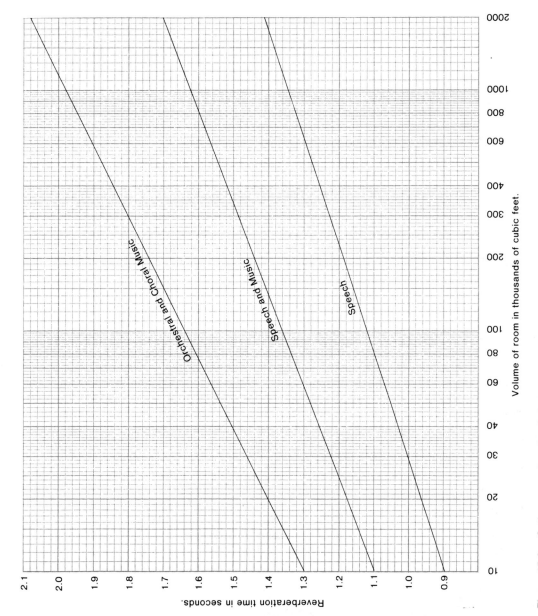

Figure 15.3. Optimum reverberation times

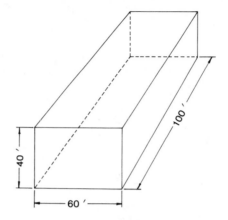

Figure 15.4. Auditorium

Table 15-B
Untreated Auditorium Surface Absorption

Surface	Area in ft²	Material	β	Sabins*
Floor and ceiling	2(60′ × 100′) = 12,000	Concrete	.01	120
End walls	2(40′ × 100′) = 4,800	Concrete block	.01	48
Side walls	2(40′ × 100′) = 8,000	Concrete block	.01	80
			Absorption of untreated surfaces = 248 sabins	

*The unit of sound absorption, the sabin, is equal to 100% absorption of one square foot of surface area.

Determination of optimum reverberation time and auditorium volume.

$$V = \text{length} \times \text{width} \times \text{height} = 100′ \times 60′ \times 40′ = 240,000 \text{ ft}^3$$

From the table of Reverberation Time versus Room Volume (Fig. 15.3) the optimum time for a room to be used for speech may be determined. Let us assume T = 1.2 seconds.

Incidentally, for this untreated auditorium, $T = \dfrac{.05\ V}{\Sigma \beta_n\ a_n} = \dfrac{.05\ (240,000)}{248} = 48.4$ seconds.

This is much too long! Obviously, a great deal of sound absorbent material will need to be added. Determination of total absorption required to attain T = 1.2

$$S = \frac{.05\ (240,000)}{1.2} = 10,000 \text{ sabins.}$$

Calculate the seating area for a total of 750 persons.

Assuming individual chairs are to be used, the approximate space required for each chair is 1.66′ wide and 2.66′ deep, or 4.42 ft², a minimum permissible. From the floor plan in Fig. 15.5, four areas, separated by aisles will be employed, each 24′ × 36.5′. Each area will provide for 14 rows of 14 seats, or a total of 750+ seats. The total of the seating sections is 3504 ft².

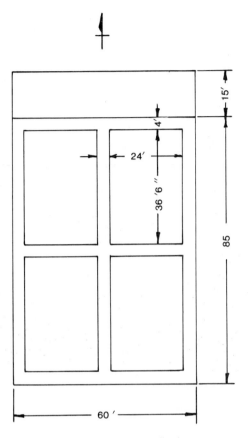

Figure 15.5. Floor plan of auditorium

Calculation of the acoustically treated surfaces. (Each is to be entered in the chart, Table 15-C.) The floor area (cork tile, carpets, people and empty seats).

To reduce the nose made by feet, the floor of the seating area will be tiled with cork. The absorption of the cork (.03) is 3504 × .03 = 105 sabins.

The absorption of the carpeted area (2496 ft^2) for 5/16″ combed pile and foam at .30 absorption is 2496 × .30 = 749 sabins.

The absorption of 500 persons, each absorbing 4 sabins, is 500 × 4 = 2000 sabins; the absorption of 250 empty chairs, each absorbing 1.75 sabins is 250 × 1.75 = 438 sabins.

The ceiling will be plastered with a rough finish (.04) to reflect speech sounds to the audience. The absorption will be 6000 × .04 = 240 sabins.

The north wall will be covered with a not-too-absorbent acoustical tile in order to reflect some speech sounds to the audience. If the tile has an absorption coefficient of .42, the absorption will be 2400 × .42 = 1008 sabins.

The south wall requires sufficient absorption to prevent a disturbing echo. Acoustical tile absorbing 70% of the sound should do the job. The absorption on the south wall then will be 2400 × .70 = 1680 sabins.

The side walls will be paneled with acoustical tile surfaces running from the floor to the ceiling, and covering two-thirds of the area. The total area of the side walls is $2 \times 40 \times 100 = 8000$ ft^2; two-thirds of this is $2/3 \times 8000 = 5333$ ft^2. If tile with an absorption coefficient of .71 is employed, the absorption will be $5333 \times .71 = 3786$ sabins. There remains the absorption of the cement block which is $2667 \times .01 = 26.7$ sabins. This is negligible and can be disregarded.

Table 15-C
Absorption of Treated Auditorium

Surface	Area	Material	β	Sabins
Floor area				
cork tile		Cork tile	.03	105
carpeted area	2496	5/16″ combed	.03	749
500 persons		pile & foam		at 4 each 2000
250 empty chairs				at 1.75 each 438
Ceiling	6000	Rough plaster	.04	240
North wall	2400	Acoustical tile	.42	1008
South wall	2400	Acoustical tile	.70	1680
Side walls	5333	Acoustical tile panels	.71	3787
				Total = 10,006 sabins (the desired amount)

If 750 people are present, T = 1.14 seconds.
If 500 people are present, T = 1.2 seconds.
If   0 people are present, T = 1.35 seconds.

This range of reverberation times is quite acceptable.

15.7 Miscellaneous Factors to Consider*

1. Air attenuates sound. This factor was not taken into consideration in the auditorium design problem. The degree of attenuation is a function of relative humidity and frequency. If the Relative Humidity = 40, about 12 sabins/1000 ft^3 are absorbed at 4 K Hz. Speech intelligibility is in a range of 250 to 4000 Hz.
2. Phase cancellation. If the direct sound from speaker to listener is out-of-phase with a reflected sound (as from a wall or the ceiling), a partial or total cancellation of that frequency will occur. This is a normal situation in an auditorium and need not be of great concern to the architect.

*Two amusing articles emphasize the importance of clothing as an acoustical absorbent. The first related to the King's College, Cambridge, England where the voluminous clothing worn by women absorbed too much sound, making the acoustics too "dead." Then, the miniskirt, well above the knee, became popular and the acoustics improved greatly. The other story is about Dr. Vern O. Knudsen, a well known physicist and acoustician at the University of California, Los Angeles. He commented that mini-skirted girls are easy on the eyes, but harder on the ears. Conventional clothing absorbs nearly twice as much sound as does the miniskirt. He admitted that the beards in the audience might help compensate for this.

3. If hearing is poor in certain parts of an auditorium, splays or clouds (small, hard reflecting panels) may be installed to reflect the sound more efficiently. If anticipated, the ceiling above the speaker area can be designed to reinforce the speaker's voice.

4. To prevent echo and room resonance (standing waves), the sound can be absorbed on one or both of the parallel walls, or the surfaces can be made irregular with angles or convex contours. This reflects the sound in many directions, thus eliminating echo without a loss in reverberation.

5. In auditoriums, lecture rooms and conference rooms, avoid absorbing very much sound on the ceiling. This reflected sound helps communication to reach the other end of the room. If, however, the ceiling is left highly reflective, the floor must then absorb sound to prevent flutter echo. An example of flutter echo may be noticed when walking on a sidewalk with a hard, reflective ceiling above.

6. Normally, flat or convex surfaces are employed. If a concave surface is to be used, it must be designed with great care to avoid focusing the sound energy in the wrong places. The radius of curvature must be considerably larger or smaller than the distance to the listener.

The reflecting surface, such as used in the band shell in the park, is intended to amplify the sound heard by the audience. Normally, a parabolic-type reflector is used, but the ellipse or sphere will provide efficient reflection of sound. Probably the least efficient reflector, and most often used, is the "billboard" reflector which reflects a large portion of the sound into the sky, lost forever to the audience. Some types of reflecting surfaces are illustrated in Fig. 15.6.

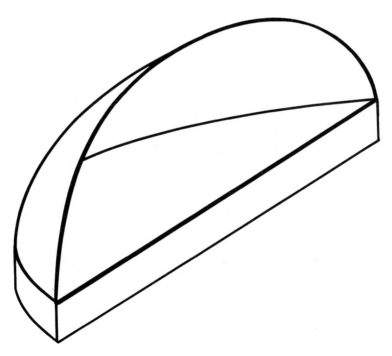

Figure 15.6A. Parabolic reflector

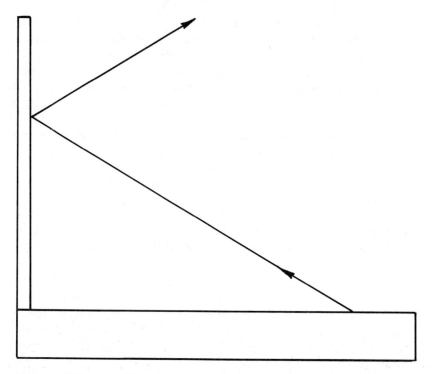

Figure 15.6B.   Billboard reflector

7. In the modern open-space offices, wall dividers may be employed to minimize the disturbing sounds. These dividers (available commercially) should consist of two isolated surfaces, perhaps mounted in rubber, and be as massive as practical. If they attenuate the sound sufficiently, one must cope with that sound going over the top of the barrier. Huygens' principle states that the sound will go around a corner, although with much less intensity. Care must be taken to prevent reflected sound from the ceiling and re-reflected from the floor. Carpets should be employed, and highly absorbent ceiling tile installed.

8. If electronic sound amplification is required, and most rooms greater than 200,000 ft^3 will require it, the speakers should be located as near the audience as possible. They can be above the audience (since the individual cannot tell where the sound source is if in the sagittal plane). If located near the microphone, they should be directed so as to prevent acoustical feedback. Directional loud speaker systems may be constructed with the speakers in a vertical line. This will cause the sound to spread horizontally covering the audience.

9. Finally, one needs to consider the following:
   a. The cost
   b. The light-reflecting characteristics
   c. The fire characteristics (fire endurance and flame spread)
   d. The durability (resistance to mechanical damage)
   e. The aesthetic characteristics

Table 15-D
Absorption of Various Materials

Materials	125 Hz	250 Hz	500 Hz	1000 Hz	2000 Hz	4000 Hz
			Coefficients			
Brick, unglazed	.03	.03	.03	.04	.05	.07
Brick, unglazed, painted	.01	.01	.02	.02	.02	.03
Carpet						
1/8″ pile height	.05	.05	.10	.20	.30	.40
1/4″ pile height	.05	.10	.15	.30	.50	.55
3/16″ combined pile & foam	.05	.10	.10	.30	.40	.50
5/16″ combined pile & foam	.05	.15	.30	.40	.50	.60
Concrete Block, painted	.10	.05	.06	.07	.09	.08
Fabrics						
Light velour, 10 oz. per sq. yd., hung straight, in contact with wall	.03	.04	.11	.17	.24	.35
Medium velour, 14 oz. per sq. yd., draped to half area	.07	.31	.49	.75	.70	.60
Heavy velour, 18 oz. per sq. yd., draped to half area	.14	.35	.55	.72	.70	.65
Floors						
Concrete or Terrazzo	.01	.01	01	.02	.02	.02
Linoleum, asphalt, rubber or cork tile on concrete	.02	.03	.03	.03	.03	.02
Wood	.15	.11	.10	.07	.06	.07
Wood parquet in asphalt on concrete	.04	.04	.07	.06	.06	.07
Glass						
1/4″, sealed, large panes	.05	.03	.02	.02	.03	.02
24 oz., operable windows in closed condition	.10	.05	.04	.03	.03	.03
Gypsum Board, 1/2″ nailed to 2 × 4's, 16″ o.c., painted	.10	.08	.05	.03	.03	.03
Marble or Glazed Tile	.01	.01	.01	.01	.02	.02
Plaster, gypsum or lime, rough finish or lath	.02	.03	.04	.05	.04	.03
Same, with smooth finish	.02	.02	.03	.04	.04	.03
Hardwood Plywood paneling 1/4″ thick, wood frame	.58	.22	.07	.04	.03	.07
Wood roof decking, tongue-and-groove cedar	.24	.19	.14	.08	.13	.10
Perforated cane fiber tile, cemented to concrete 1″ thick	.14	.20	.76	.79	.58	.37
Acoustical plaster 1″ thick	.25	.45	.78	.92	.89	.87
Celotex Safetone perforated mineral fiber tile 5/8″	.61	.57	.69	.99	.83	.51
Seats, lightly upholstered with leather, plastic, etc. (sabins)			1.5-2.0 sabins			
Audience seated (sabins)	2.5-4.0	3.5-5.0	4.0-5.5	4.5-6.5	5.0-7.0	4.5-7.0
Air, Sabins per 1000 cubic feet @ 50% R.H.				.90	2.3	7.2

For the initial calculations, the absorption at 500 Hertz is used.
Information provided by Ceilings and Interior Systems Contractors Association, Glenview, Illinois, and reprinted with permission.

Review Questions for Chapter 15. Architectural Acoustics

1. What is the minimum distance to a flat reflecting wall which might produce a disturbing echo?

2. Describe two ways echo in a large room can be solved.

3. What is reverberation? What is the formula to determine the reverberation time?

4. What is one Sabin of sound absorption?

5. How may one determine the optimum reverberation time for a given room?

6. Normally, does a room to be used for speech require a longer or shorter reverberation time than a room to be used for music?

7. How may the reverberation time of a room be altered or controlled?

8. Normally, should concave or convex surfaces within a room be avoided? Which?

9. How can an auditorium be made less sensitive to audience size with respect to the reverberation time?

10. Normally, in a room to be used for speech, should the absorbent tile be placed on the ceiling or on the walls?

11. Does heavy carpeting on a felt pad absorb high frequency sounds better than low? What about hard, non-porous surfaces like plywood?

12. What are splays or clouds? How and why are they used?

13. .What is meant by "sound isolation"? What are the usual methods for accomplishing sound isolation? About how many decibels attenuation might one expect of a cement block wall?

14. What is staggered stud construction? Does acoustical absorbent tile provide satisfactory sound isolation?

15. What is impact sound? How may it be eliminated or reduced?

16. How may windows be constructed so as to isolate sound? What about doors?

17. How can one prevent sound from being transmitted through ventilator ducts?

18. How is "white noise" employed to maintain confidentiality?

19. What is flutter echo? How may it be eliminated?

20. Describe some reflecting surfaces which may be employed as a band shell?

21. What does the "coefficient of absorption" represent?

CHAPTER **16**

Sound Pollution

Sound pollution is a newly recognized hazard, and one about which we have relatively little information at present. It is well established that high intensity sound, above perhaps 85 dB, can permanently damage the hearing mechanism if heard over a prolonged period of time. We are all aware of the sources of very intense sound, such as artillery fire, unmuffled exhaust systems on cars, airplanes, tractors, motorcycles, lawnmowers and chain saws. Also, pneumatic hammers, factory machinery, heavy equipment including farm machinery, and subway or elevated trains produce noise at a dangerously high level. The sound produced by a space rocket on take-off is so intense it can kill anyone nearby.

You may have noticed that members of the ground crew outside a jet airplane, particularly the turbojet, wear padded earphones. These serve two purposes: provide for communication and reduce the intensity of the sound. Those involved in a job which requires that they be near high intensity sound for prolonged periods of time should protect themselves with ear plugs or some other sound attenuating device. Cotton plugs will do little good unless impregnated with some material like beeswax. It is not necessary to absorb all of the sound, but merely to reduce its intensity to a safe and comfortable level, perhaps 85 dB or less. The "Rock" musician should stand in back of his speaker system and wear ear plugs. The audience will get the brunt of this damaging sound, but for shorter periods of time so probably little damage will result. Also, they can leave the room, or move away from the PA system if they wish. Not so for the performer!

Audiometric tests of entering freshmen college students indicate the incidence of high frequency hearing loss is on the increase. A great many of these cases were high school Rock Band performers.

Some thought should be given to the symphony orchestra or band performer. Actual measurements of the sound intensity in the group reaches the danger level.

It is known that a very intense sound will actually destroy tissue cells which, in the hearing mechanism, can cause deafness—even total deafness. The intense sound can dislodge the cilia or damage other cells within the mechanism. The damage is principally to the higher frequencies so it will badly affect the hearing or understanding of speech.

Damage to the hearing mechanism is not the only adverse effect on the human body. Among other things, intense sounds reportedly affect the blood pressure, the heartbeat rhythm, metabolism, sexual capacity, sleep patterns, increases the blood cholesterol level, and incidence of ulcers, indigestion, heart disease and general stress which is linked with mental illness. It can disturb and cause changes in the unborn fetus.

People associate loud sound with power. The adolescent is particularly fond of a noisy automobile because it makes him feel powerful and gives him a much sought-after status with his friends.

Pressure must be brought to bear on the manufacturers of machinery, for it is possible to design machines that produce little sound. It is easier to design a machine to operate quietly than to try to absorb the sound a noisy machine makes. The chief offenders in a community are the lawn mower (dangerous particularly to the operator), motorcycle, automobiles with defective mufflers, and the semi-trailers, particularly when accelerating or decelerating. You have noticed the intense sound produced as a semi-trailer passes you on the highway, or as it approaches or leaves a "stop" intersection. Industrial sound can be minimized with improved equipment. If it is not possible or feasible to quiet the equipment, strict regulations should be enforced to install sound barriers around the sound source, or have the personnel protect themselves with ear plugs or other devices which will attenuate the sound to a safe level, less than 85 dB. The labor unions should make every effort to protect the worker's hearing.

The kitchen is the noisiest room in the house with its loud mixer, blender, automatic dish-washer, trash compactor, garbage disposal, operating in a room with hard, reflecting surfaces. The maximum of sound absorbent material should be installed in the kitchen, even appropriate car-peting. This will be of great benefit to the housewife who spends so much time in the kitchen.

It has been reported that excessive consumption of alcohol reduces the efficiency of the protective device in our hearing mechanism to loud sounds.

In some instances, acoustical pollution is confused with the psychological reaction to certain sounds; therefore, it is necessary to consider the reasons for complaints when establishing com-munity sound abatement programs. One elderly lady complained that the sound intensity of a Rock Band, playing on the patio of a local tavern a city block from her home, was excessive. Actual measurements revealed that the band's sound level at her home was less than that made by a quietly operating automobile slowly passing her house. Doubtless, she objected to Rock music, to taverns, and to college students, so her annoyance was not due to the sound level, but rather to an intense dislike for the activity. It is quite possible that a symphony orchestra playing an evening concert on the patio would have been enjoyed thoroughly. The police had no choice, however, but to stop the band from playing outdoors.

Most of us do not have access to a dB meter. Therefore, a "rule of thumb": if the sound is so loud that you must shout to be understood, it is probably going to damage your hearing process after a period of time. Unfortunately, there is no cure for the noise-induced hearing loss. Once you have lost your hearing, you have lost it for the rest of your life!

With the continual rise in ambient sound conditions, a frightening future lies ahead unless this hazard is recognized and something is done to protect us from the adverse effects. It is only recently that the sounds around us reached intensity levels that are harmful. Therefore, research in this area is in its infancy and we are just now learning about the dangers. What will they be after the next decade?

Review Questions for Chapter 16. Sound Pollution

1. Sound pollution is referred to as both physical and psychological. What does this mean?

2. What are the chief sources of sound pollution?

3. Above what decibel level will sound permanently affect the hearing mechanism?

4. For those working in an atmosphere of high intensity sound, what precautions can they take to prevent hearing damage?

5. If sound is sufficiently intense, can it kill? Name one example of such sound.

6. What are the reported decibel levels for (a) a quiet whisper, (b) an average office, (c) a jack hammer or rock band?

7. Besides the destruction of tissue cells, what other detrimental effects does intense sound have upon the human being?

8. Which is the noisiest room in the average house?

9. If the hearing mechanism is damaged due to intense sound, will it heal after a period of time?

10. What "rule-of-thumb" can be applied to ascertain whether a sound is dangerously intense?

11. What recommendations do you have to help solve the ever increasing problem of sound pollution?

12. Is polluting sound dangerous to the unborn child?

Appendixes

Table of Sines

Angle	Sine		Angle	Sine		Angle	Sine
0°	0.000						
1	0.018		31°	0.515		61°	0.875
2	0.035		32	0.530		62	0.883
3	0.052		33	0.545		63	0.891
4	0.070		34	0.559		64	0.899
5	0.087		35	0.574		65	0.906
6	0.105		36	0.588		66	0.914
7	0.122		37	0.602		67	0.921
8	0.139		38	0.616		68	0.927
9	0.156		39	0.629		69	0.934
10	0.174		40	0.643		70	0.940
11	0.191		41	0.656		71	0.946
12	0.208		42	0.669		72	0.951
13	0.225		43	0.682		73	0.956
14	0.242		44	0.695		74	0.961
15	0.259		45	0.707		75	0.966
16	0.276		46	0.719		76	0.970
17	0.292		47	0.731		77	0.974
18	0.309		48	0.743		78	0.978
19	0.326		49	0.755		79	0.982
20	0.342		50	0.766		80	0.985
21	0.358		51	0.777		81	0.988
22	0.375		52	0.788		82	0.990
23	0.391		53	0.799		83	0.993
24	0.407		54	0.809		84	0.995
25	0.423		55	0.819		85	0.996
26	0.438		56	0.829		86	0.998
27	0.454		57	0.839		87	0.999
28	0.470		58	0.848		88	0.999
29	0.485		59	0.857		89	1.000
30	0.500		60	0.866		90	1.000

Graph Relating Temperatures Fahrenheit and Centigrade (Celsius)

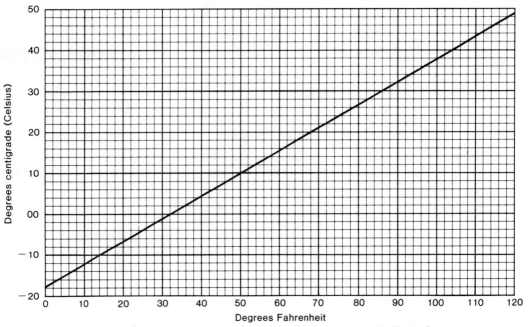

Graph relating temperatures Fahrenheit and centigrade (Celsius)

Pipe Length versus Fundamental Frequency in Hz.

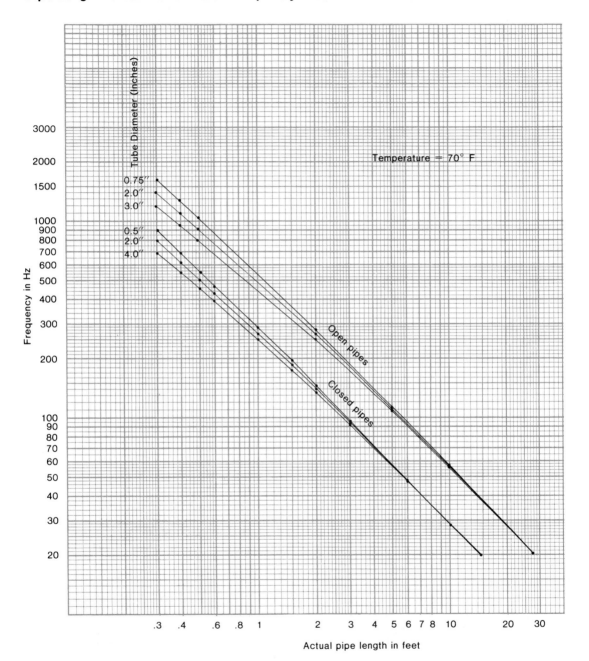

Formulas for the Square, Triangular and Sawtooth Waves

Square wave $y = \dfrac{4E}{\pi}\left(\cos\theta - \dfrac{\cos 3\,\theta}{3} + \dfrac{\cos 5\,\theta}{5} - \dfrac{\cos 7\,\theta}{7} + \cdots\right)$

Triangular wave $y = \dfrac{8E}{\pi^2}\left(\cos\theta + \dfrac{\cos 3\,\theta}{9} + \dfrac{\cos 5\,\theta}{25} + \cdots\right)$

Sawtooth wave $y = \dfrac{2E}{\pi}\left(\sin\theta - \dfrac{\sin 2\,\theta}{2} + \dfrac{\sin 3\,\theta}{3} - \dfrac{\sin 4\,\theta}{4} + \cdots\right)$

Table of Logarithms

Using Tables of Logarithms

Scientific notation

It is possible to represent a number by using powers of 10. In other words, $100 = 10 \times 10 = 10^2$, where the power, 2, equals the number of zeros. It would be written $1 \times 10^2 = 100$. Another example: $1{,}000{,}000 = 10^6$.

Logarithms

The logarithm of a number, N, is the power to which 10 must be raised to obtain that number, N. Therefore, in the above example, $100 = 10^2$, the logarithm of $100 = 2$. Not all are so easily determined. For most numbers, a table of logarithms is employed. The table on pages 172 and 173 gives the logs for numbers from 10 to 100.

To determine the log of a number, first write the number of digits to the left of the decimal point, and subtract 1. This is known as the characteristic. Then, look in the table for the log of the number, and record that to the right of the decimal point. This is known as the mantissa.

Example: log 2 = 0.3010. The characteristics is $1 - 1 = 0$; from the table, the mantissa is .3010

also,   log 30 = 1.4771. The characteristic is $2 - 1 = 1$; from the table, locate the first digit, 3, in the left hand column, then move to the right, horizontally, until you come to the column headed by the second digit, 0. The mantissa, the three-digit number 0.4771, plus the characteristic 1.0, is the logarithm which equals 1.4771.

To multiply two numbers, add their logarithms. Then, from the log table, look up the answer.

Example: $2 \times 30 = \log^2 + \log 30 = 0.3010 + 1.4771 = 1.778$. From the table, the digits to the right of the decimal point, .4771, gives the number 6.; the location of the decimal point is given by adding 1 to the number left of the decimal point. In this case, $1 + 1 = 2$. Therefore, there will be two digits to the left of the decimal point, which provides the answer, 60.

To divide, subtract the log of the denominator from the log of the numerator.

Example: $\dfrac{30}{2}$ = log 30 − log 2 = 1.4771 − 0.3010 = 1.1761

From the log table, the answer is 15.0

To raise a number to the power n, multiply the log by the power.

Example: 30^2 = 2 × log 30 = 2 × 1.4771 = 2.954

From the log table, the answer is 900.

To take the nth root of a number, divide the log by n.

Example: $\sqrt[2]{30}$ = $\dfrac{\log 30}{2}$ = $\dfrac{1.4771}{2}$ = 0.7385

From the log table, the answer is approximately 5.4^7

For more accurate calculations, a 5-place logarithm table should be used, or an electronic calculator.

Four Place Common Logarithms
$\log_{10} N$

N	0	1	2	3	4	5	6	7	8	9
10	0000	0043	0086	0128	0170	0212	0253	0294	0334	0374
11	0414	0453	0492	0531	0569	0607	0645	0682	0719	0755
12	0792	0828	0864	0899	0934	0969	1004	1038	1072	1106
13	1139	1173	1206	1239	1271	1303	1335	1367	1399	1430
14	1461	1492	1523	1553	1584	1614	1644	1673	1703	1732
15	1761	1790	1818	1847	1875	1903	1931	1959	1987	2014
16	2041	2068	2095	2122	2148	2175	2201	2227	2253	2279
17	2304	2330	2355	2380	2405	2430	2455	2480	2504	2529
18	2553	2577	2601	2625	2648	2672	2695	2718	2742	2765
19	2788	2810	2833	2856	2878	2900	2923	2945	2967	2989
20	3010	3032	3054	3075	3096	3118	3139	3160	3181	3201
21	3222	3243	3263	3284	3304	3324	3345	3365	3385	3404
22	3424	3444	3464	3483	3502	3522	3541	3560	3579	3598
23	3617	3636	3655	3674	3692	3711	3729	3747	3766	3784
24	3802	3820	3838	3856	3874	3892	3909	3927	3945	3962
25	3979	3997	4014	4031	4048	4065	4082	4099	4116	4133
26	4150	4166	4183	4200	4216	4232	4249	4265	4281	4298
27	4314	4330	4346	4362	4378	4393	4409	4425	4440	4456
28	4472	4487	4502	4518	4533	4548	4564	4579	4594	4609
29	4624	4639	4654	4669	4683	4698	4713	4728	4742	4757
30	4771	4786	4800	4814	4829	4843	4857	4871	4886	4900
31	4914	4928	4942	4955	4969	4983	4997	5011	5024	5038
32	5051	5065	5079	5092	5105	5119	5132	5145	5159	5172
33	5185	5198	5211	5224	5237	5250	5263	5276	5289	5302
34	5315	5328	5340	5353	5366	5378	5391	5403	5416	5428
35	5441	5453	5465	5478	5490	5502	5514	5527	5539	5551
36	5563	5575	5587	5599	5611	5623	5635	5647	5658	5670
37	5682	5694	5705	5717	5729	5740	5752	5763	5775	5786
38	5798	5809	5821	5832	5843	5855	5866	5877	5888	5899
39	5911	5922	5933	5944	5955	5966	5977	5988	5999	6010
40	6021	6031	6042	6053	6064	6075	6085	6096	6107	6117
41	6128	6138	6149	6160	6170	6180	6191	6201	6212	6222
42	6232	6243	6253	6263	6274	6284	6294	6304	6314	6325
43	6335	6345	6355	6365	6375	6385	6395	6405	6415	6425
44	6435	6444	6454	6464	6474	6484	6493	6503	6513	6522
45	6532	6542	6551	6561	6571	6580	6590	6599	6609	6618
46	6628	6637	6646	6656	6665	6675	6684	6693	6702	6712
47	6721	6730	6739	6749	6758	6767	6776	6785	6794	6803
48	6812	6821	6830	6839	6848	6857	6866	6875	6884	6893
49	6902	6911	6920	6928	6937	6946	6955	6964	6972	6981
50	6990	6998	7007	7016	7024	7033	7042	7050	7059	7067
51	7076	7084	7093	7101	7110	7118	7126	7135	7143	7152
52	7160	7168	7177	7185	7193	7202	7210	7218	7226	7235
53	7243	7251	7259	7267	7275	7284	7292	7300	7308	7316
54	7324	7332	7340	7348	7356	7364	7372	7380	7388	7396
N	0	1	2	3	4	5	6	7	8	9

This table was taken from *Mathematical Handbook of Formulas and Tables* by Murray R. Spiegel. Schaum's Outline Series, McGraw-Hill Co.

Four Place Common Logarithms
$\log_{10} N$—*Continued*

N	0	1	2	3	4	5	6	7	8	9
55	7404	7412	7419	7427	7435	7443	7451	7459	7466	7474
56	7482	7490	7497	7505	7513	7520	7528	7536	7543	7551
57	7559	7566	7574	7582	7589	7597	7604	7612	7619	7627
58	7634	7642	7649	7657	7664	7672	7679	7686	7694	7701
59	7709	7716	7723	7731	7738	7745	7752	7760	7767	7774
60	7782	7789	7796	7803	7810	7818	7825	7832	7839	7846
61	7853	7860	7868	7875	7882	7889	7896	7903	7910	7917
62	7924	7931	7938	7945	7952	7959	7966	7973	7980	7987
63	7993	8000	8007	8014	8021	8028	8035	8041	8048	8055
64	8062	8069	8075	8082	8089	8096	8102	8109	8116	8122
65	8129	8136	8142	8149	8156	8162	8169	8176	8182	8189
66	8195	8202	8209	8215	8222	8228	8235	8241	8248	8254
67	8261	8267	8274	8280	8287	8293	8299	8306	8312	8319
68	8325	8331	8338	8344	8351	8357	8363	8370	8376	8382
69	8388	8395	8401	8407	8414	8420	8426	8432	8439	8445
70	8451	8457	8463	8470	8476	8482	8488	8494	8500	8506
71	8513	8519	8525	8531	8537	8543	8549	8555	8561	8567
72	8573	8579	8585	8591	8597	8603	8609	8615	8621	8627
73	8633	8639	8645	8651	8657	8663	8669	8675	8681	8686
74	8692	8698	8704	8710	8716	8722	8727	8733	8739	8745
75	8751	8756	8762	8768	8774	8779	8785	8791	8797	8802
76	8808	8814	8820	8825	8831	8837	8842	8848	8854	8859
77	8865	8871	8876	8882	8887	8893	8899	8904	8910	8915
78	8921	8927	8932	8938	8943	8949	8954	8960	8965	8971
79	8976	8982	8987	8993	8998	9004	9009	9015	9020	9025
80	9031	9036	9042	9047	9053	9058	9063	9069	9074	9079
81	9085	9090	9096	9101	9106	9112	9117	9122	9128	9133
82	9138	9143	9149	9154	9159	9165	9170	9175	9180	9186
83	9191	9196	9201	9206	9212	9217	9222	9227	9232	9238
84	9243	9248	9253	9258	9263	9269	9274	9279	9284	9289
85	9294	9299	9304	9309	9315	9320	9325	9330	9335	9340
86	9345	9350	9355	9360	9365	9370	9375	9380	9385	9390
87	9395	9400	9405	9410	9415	9420	9425	9430	9435	9440
88	9445	9450	9455	9460	9465	9469	9474	9479	9484	9489
89	9494	9499	9504	9509	9513	9518	9523	9528	9533	9538
90	9542	9547	9552	9557	9562	9566	9571	9576	9581	9586
91	9590	9595	9600	9605	9609	9614	9619	9624	9628	9633
92	9638	9643	9647	9652	9657	9661	9666	9671	9675	9680
93	9685	9689	9694	9699	9703	9708	9713	9717	9722	9727
94	9731	9736	9741	9745	9750	9754	9759	9763	9768	9773
95	9777	9782	9786	9791	9795	9800	9805	9809	9814	9818
96	9823	9827	9832	9836	9841	9845	9850	9854	9859	9863
97	9868	9872	9877	9881	9886	9890	9894	9899	9903	9908
98	9912	9917	9921	9926	9930	9934	9939	9943	9948	9952
99	9956	9961	9965	9969	9974	9978	9983	9987	9991	9996
N	0	1	2	3	4	5	6	7	8	9

Glossary

Abscissa—The horizontal distance from the y-axis to a point or curve.

Absolute pitch—The ability to provide the pitch name for a sound without reference to a known pitch.

Acoustical feedback—A fairly pure tone produced when the microphone is too near the loud speaker.

Amplitude—The maximum vertical height of a sine wave, or the maximum displacement of a vibrating body.

Angle of incidence—The angle that a straight line (representing the propagation of a sound from the source to a reflecting surface), makes with a normal to the surface (the perpendicular to the surface).

Angle of reflection—The angle that a straight line (representing the reflection of a sound), makes with a normal to the surface (the perpendicular to the surface).

Antinode—The point of maximum amplitude of a vibrating body, located midway between two nodal points.

Attenuate—To reduce in magnitude, like a volume control.

Audio spectrum—A graph of the distribution of acoustical energy within the hearing range.

Audiogram—A graph of the hearing response, normally at the auditory threshold.

Auditory threshold—The minimum perceptible intensity.

Aural harmonics—Harmonics generated within the hearing mechanism but not existing outside the ear.

Baffle—A solid surface employed to stop or deflect sound.

Batter head—The membrane on a drum that is struck.

Beat—A periodic change in tonal intensity due to two tones of different frequency interacting to produce a cycle of interference then reinforcement due to the change in phase.

Beat tone—A tone resulting from beats occurring about 20 times per second or more. This tone does not exist as a separate entity. Other names for the beat tone are: subjective tone, difference or summation tone, heterodyne tone, combination tone, etc.

Binaural sound—Sounds heard with two ears. This is true directional sound, requiring two microphones, two amplifiers and two earphones.

Bore—The longitudinal hole of any given shape inside of an instrument like an oboe.

Bridge—An object over which a taut string is stretched, terminating the vibration at one end. It also serves, on a violin, to conduct the sound to the resonator.

Cambiata—In acoustics it refers to the changing voice.

Castrato—A male soprano, castrated before puberty to retain his soprano range and quality. This was an 18th century practice.

Celesta—A musical instrument consisting of a set of metal plates, struck with hammers which are activated by a keyboard.

Cent—One-hundredth of a semitone.

Chord—A combination of two or more musical tones sounded together.

Cilia—Short hair-like structures in the inner ear, terminating with the auditory nerve.

Closed tube—A resonant tube, closed at one end.

Cochlea—A spiral-shaped cavity containing the inner ear.

Coefficient of absorption—The amount of sound absorbed by one square foot of surface.

Coloratura—A voice capable of performing trills and florid, ornate passages.

Combination tones—Beat tones, produced by sounding two or more tones of different frequency together.

Complemental air—The volume of air which may be inspired in excess of the tidal air capacity.

Complex wave—Any waveshape (as seen on the oscilloscope) which is not a sine wave, being made up of more than one pure tone.

Contralto—A female voice of heavy quality and low pitch.

Costal region—The rib cage.

Crystal microphone—A microphone containing a thin slice of crystal which, when deformed mechanically, produces a voltage between the two sides.

Crescendo pedal—A pedal on the pipe organ which changes the loudness of the tone.

Damper—A felt pad on a piano which, when pressed against the strings, stops them from vibrating.

Dark noise—Noise with most of the acoustical energy of low frequency.

Decibel—A tenth of a Bel. A unit of sound intensity.

Diatonic scale—The major or minor scale, containing five whole tone and two semitone intervals.

Diffraction of sound—The bending of sound waves around obstacles in their path. It explains how sound can be heard around a corner.

Distortion—The changing of a waveshape or quality from its original condition.

Doppler effect—The change in pitch of a sound due to the relative motion of the sound source and the listener.

Dramatic tone—An intense vocal or instrumental tone, usually with a prominent intensity vibrato.

Dynamic microphone or speaker—A microphone or loud speaker requiring a permanent magnet and moving coil for its operation.

Echo—The intelligible reflection of sound.

Edge tone—A tone produced by blowing against a sharp edge as with the flute.

Embouchure—The mouthpiece of a wind instrument or the muscular control of the lips when playing a wind instrument.

Enharmonic equivalent—Two notes with different names, but sounding the same pitch such as B# and C on the piano.

Equally tempered scale—A scale whose pitches are adjusted slightly so as to sound as well in tune in one key as in any other key. This permits modulation from one key to another without retuning the piano.

Eustachian tube—A tube leading from the middle ear cavity to the oral cavity to maintain atmospheric pressure in the middle ear.

Explosive consonants—Those consonants such as "k," "p" and "t" in which the air pressure is built up, then released suddenly.

Exponential horn—The flared end of a trumpet.

f-hole—The f-shaped hole in the belly of a violin. An opening in the resonant cavity to allow the sound to escape.

Flat (♭)—A flat lowers the pitch of a tone one semitone, to the next lower pitch on the piano keyboard.

Formant—A region of resonance on the frequency scale.

Frequency—Cycles or vibrations per second; Hertz.

Frequency discrimination—The ability to discriminate between two tones of nearly the same frequency without requiring a pitch judgement.

Frets—Raised lines crossing the fingerboard that predetermine the vibrating length of a string.

Fundamental—The lowest pitch resonated. Equivalent to the first partial.

Harmonics—Tones whose frequencies are integral multiples of the fundamental frequency.

Harmonic spectrum—The amount of energy in each harmonic of a complex tone.

Harp theory—An early explanation of the theory of hearing in which the cilia responded in resonance to frequencies over the length of the basilar membrane, much as the strings of a harp would vibrate sympathetically.

Hertz (Hz)—The number of vibrations or cycles per second.

Hill-and-dale—A vertical cut in a phonograph recording.

Huygens' principle—Explanation of diffraction. Every point on a wave front may be considered a new sound source.

Idiophones—Percussion instruments made of a solid, resonant material.

Impact sound—Sound made by an impact, such as hammering.

Incisors—The four anterior teeth in each jaw.

Inharmonic overtones—Overtones which are not harmonics. Frequencies of inharmonic overtones are not whole number multiples of a fundamental.

Inner ear—The portion of the hearing process lying within the cochlea, and containing the auditory nerve endings.

Integers—Positive or negative whole numbers

Interference—When two or more sound waves are not in phase, and bring about a degree of cancellation.

Interval—The number of scale tones existing between two pitches.

Intonation—The pitch of a tone related to the key.

J.N.D. or J.P.D.—Just Noticeable Difference or Just Perceptible Difference.

Just scale—The "in tune" scale whose pitches are based on the pitches of the partials or harmonics.

Kinesthesia—The sensation of movement or strain in muscles. Muscle sense.

Kymograph—An instrument for graphically recording respiration, heart-beat, etc. A recording voltmeter.

Labia—Lips. Form the vowels "oh" and "oo."

Laryngoscope—A device inserted into the oral cavity to examine the larynx.

Larynx—The voice box. The vocal folds which produce the vocal sound.

Ligature—A metal band that secures the reed on a clarinet.

Lissajous figure—A design made by two frequencies vibrating at right angles to one another. The ratio of the number of loops across the top of the design to the number of loops on the side is the same as the frequency ratio. They indicate Just intonation.

Longitudinal wave—A wave in which the vibration is along the axis of the vibrating member. A sound wave in the air is a longitudinal wave.

Lyric—A classification of a voice which is light in quality, high in pitch, and normally has a pitch vibrato.

Manometer—An instrument for measuring air pressure. A U-shaped glass tube half filled with a liquid.

Manuals—The keyboards on a pipe organ.

Masking—The drowning out of one tone by another.

Mass—Similar to weight though not dependent on the force of gravity.

Membranophones—Percussion instruments that employ a membrane as their sound source; drums are membranophones.

Mezzo (soprano)—A soprano of medium pitch and quality. Most women are mezzo sopranos.

Middle ear—That portion of the mechanism located between the tympanum and the cochlea, containing the ossicles.

Minor scale—There are three minor scales: natural, harmonic and melodic. The principal identifying characteristic is the lowered third of the scale containing three semitone intervals, as compared with the major third which has four semitone intervals.

Modulation—In music, modulation means change from one key to another.

Musical sound—A sound with identifiable pitch, in contrast to noise which has no identifiable pitch.

Mute—An object which clamps on the violin bridge, increasing its mass, to alter the tone quality and reduce the sound intensity. Other instruments have mutes such as the trumpet mute which fits inside the end of the instrument (the bell).

Nasal cavity—An enlarged portion of the respiratory path, located above the palate.

Natural (♮)—This symbol cancels the effect of a flat or sharp.

Node (nodule)—In a vibrating sound source, like a violin string, the node is the point of little or no motion which exists when playing harmonics. Node, or nodule, also refers to a knob or protuberance on the vocal folds, resembling a wart.

Noise—The result of random, aperiodic sound impulses, such as is produced by scraping sandpaper. Noise does not produce an identifiable pitch.

Nut—A raised part at the end of a vibrating string furthest from the bridge. The nut and bridge determine the length of a vibrating open string.

Octave—A musical interval produced by tones whose frequency ratio is 2:1. The first and eighth tone of our scale sound an octave.

Omni-directional—Equally responsive in all directions, such as an omni-directional microphone.

Open tube—A resonant tube, open at both ends. An antinode is produced at both ends.

Optimum—The best. Note the difference between optimum and maximum.

Oral cavity—The mouth cavity.

Ordinate—The vertical distance from the x-axis to a point or curve.

Oscillator—A mechanical or electrical device which produces vibrations. An audio oscillator produces vibrations whose frequencies are within the hearing range.

Ossicles—The three small bones (hammer, anvil and stirrup), located in the middle ear. They conduct the sound from the "ear drum" to the middle ear, amplifying the intensity of the sound by leverage.

Outer ear—That portion of the ear which collects the sound and conducts it to the tympanum.

Oval window—One of two membranes terminating the cochlea. The stirrup is attached to the oval window.

Overtone—In a complex tone, any tone whose frequency is greater than that of the fundamental. They need not be harmonics.

Overwinding—To increase the mass (weight) of a string in order to lower its frequency without altering the tension, the tension string is wound with one or more layers of wire.

Pain threshold—The intensity-frequency contour representing the maximum loudness perceived. Any further increase in intensity will be felt and painful.

Palate—The roof of the mouth, made up of the hard and soft palates.

Parabola or paraboloid—A curve of the form $y = ax^2$. The shape of a spotlight reflector. It has one focal point.

Partial—A pure tone which is a part of a complex tone. Similar to harmonic. The first partial is the same as the fundamental.

Pedal tone—The fundamental, or lowest pitch of a partial or harmonic series.

Pharynx—A tube or cavity, and its associated parts, leading from the vocal folds to the nasal cavity. It is divided into three parts: laryngeal pharynx, oral pharynx, and nasopharynx. It serves as an important vocal resonator and determines to a large extent the basic quality of the voice.

Phase—The relative timing of two tones. If operating together, they are said to be in phase. If operating one-half cycle apart, they are said to be out-of-phase. Phase is measured in degrees, indicating the degree they are out-of-phase.

Phon (phon contour)—The apparent loudness of a tone. If the loudness of a tone of any frequency is made equal to the loudness of a 1000 Hz tone, they have the same phon level, represented by the dB value of the 1000 Hz tone. If a great many tones are adjusted in loudness to equal the loudness of a 1000 Hz tone, and the results graphed, the smooth curve connecting the points will represent an equal-loudness or phon contour.

Phonation—A vocal tone in which the larynx is vibrating.

Pitch—The highness of lowness of a tone, identified by a letter name such as A$\#$ or E^b.

Pitch discrimination—The ability of a person to indicate which of two tones, whose frequencies are nearly the same, is the higher or lower.

Pizzicato—Plucking the string to make it vibrate.

Place theory—The theory in which the pitch perception is based on the "place" along the basilar membrane an acoustical disturbance is maximized. This theory explains, only in part, the reception and identification of pitch.

Plectrum—The object employed to pluck strings.

Port—An opening, window or door. A hole cut in a loud speaker enclosure.

Print through—Due to the intensity of the magnetism and the thinness of the acetate, a magnetic tape can magnetize adjacent turns causing a pre and post echo.

Pure tone—A tone produced by single frequency of sinusoidal waveshape.

Pythagorean scale—A scale, composed of tones whose frequencies are derived, when ascending in pitch, by intervals of a fifth: $f_2/f_1 = 1.5$.

Quadraphonic—A multi-channel sound in which two additional speakers are placed in the rear corners of the room to simulate the normal reflection heard by the audience. It is also called "surround sound."

Real tone—A tone of audible frequency that exists before entering the hearing process, in contrast to the subjective tone.

Reed pipes—Organ pipes in which the sound source is a vibrating reed.

Refraction of sound—The bending of sound due to its propagation through air of different temperatures.

Registration—The pre-setting of organ stops to select those which are to sound. It is a type of "programming."

Reinforcement—The adding of two in phase sounds resulting in an increase in loudness.

Relative pitch—The ability to provide the pitch name for a sound by relating it to a recently heard, known pitch.

Residual air—That volume of air which still remains in the lungs after complete expiration.

Residual magnetism—That magnetism which remains after the magnetizing unit has been removed.

Resonance—The predisposition of a body or air cavity to vibrate. It is not necessary that a sound is being produced.

Reverberation—The multiple reflection of sound due to many highly reflective surfaces in a room.

Reverberation time—The time it takes for a sound to die out to one-millionth of its initial intensity, 60 dB.

Rosin—A hard substance made from pine resin. It is applied to the bow of stringed instruments causing it to stick to the string.

Round window—One of two membranes terminating the cochlea. Its function is to permit the non-compressible liquid within the cochlea to move.

Sabin—The unit of sound absorption. One sabin equals the 100% absorption of one square foot of surface.

Sagittal plane—That plane which divides the head, left and right. Every point on the sagittal plane is equi-distant to the two ears.

Saw-tooth wave—A waveshape resembling a saw-tooth. It rises at a constant rate, then drops instantly to rise again. It is composed of all the partials.

Semitone—The smallest pitch interval that can be played on the piano.

Sforzando piston—A tone or chord played with force—explosively. Depressing the piston causes all the pipes to sound.

Sharp (#)—A sharp raises the pitch of a tone one semitone, to the next higher pitch on the piano keyboard.

Sine wave—A periodic oscillation, varying in a smooth up-and-down manner much like the calm waves on water. It is a circular function and best described by the trigonometric function, $y = a \sin x$. If the output of a loud speaker varies in this manner, a pure tone is heard.

Soprano—A female voice of light quality and high pitch. This describes the voices of most women.

Sound—In this book, sound is defined as "that which is heard."

Sound post—A short wooden dowel wedged between the belly and back of a stringed instrument. It serves two purposes: to acoustically connect the belly and back surfaces, and to help prevent cracking the belly due to the force of the strings transmitted through the bridge.

Sounding board—A large board, similar to plywood, which serves as the vibrating resonator in a piano. It amplifies the sound.

Spirometer—A device for measuring air volume (lung capacity).

Splay or cloud—A small suspended reflecting surface, to direct sound into otherwise acoustically dead portions of an auditorium.

Square wave—A waveshape which progresses from a constant positive value to a constant negative value instantaneously. It is composed of all the odd-numbered partials.

Standing wave—A wave, reflected from two parallel walls repeatedly, with the amplitude being constant at any point along its axis. This will happen when the room is resonant to the sound.

Stereophonic sound—Directional sound based on loudness. It is a synthetic directional sound system, binaural being the true system.

Stop—A "valve" on a pipe organ which allows air to activate a given set of pipes.

Stroboconn—A stroboscopic, electronic device which measures tempered frequencies.

Subjective harmonics—The same as aural harmonics.

Subsonic—Vibrations below about 20 Hz. Below the hearing range, though felt.

Supplemental air—That volume of air which may be expired below the tidal air capacity.

Sympathetic vibrations—Vibrations produced in one body due to similar vibrations sounding in another body.

Synthesis—Combining tones (partials) to form a single tone with a given pitch and quality.

Tempered scale—The piano scale in which the pitches have been adjusted to sound as well in tune in one key as in any other key.

Tendency pitches—Tones with pitches which we feel must move up or down in pitch, such as the seventh tone of the scale moving up to the eighth tone.

Tenor—A male voice of light quality and high pitch.

Thorax—The upper portion of the body enclosed by the ribs.

Threshold of audibility—See Auditory threshold.

Tidal Air—That volume of air employed during quiet respiration.

Timpani—Kettle drums.

Tom-tom—A two headed drum, like the snare drum without the snares.

Tonality—The relationships existing between the tones of a scale.

Tone—Any sound considered with reference to pitch, quality, intensity and duration. Noise is not considered tone because it lacks an identifiable pitch.

Trachea—A tube leading from the larynx to the bronchi.

Transducer—A device that converts one form of energy into another form such as a microphone which converts acoustical energy into electric energy.

Traps—A collection of objects, used in the percussion section to create special effects.

Triad—A three-tone chord.

Tympanum—A membrane separating the outer ear from the middle ear; ear drum.

Ultrasonics—A sound whose frequency is above the audible limit.

Unvoiced consonants—Those consonants in which the larynx does not vibrate. No phonation.

Uvula—A small, fleshy protuberance hanging down from the velum.

Valve—A device that inserts a short section of tubing in a brass instrument to lengthen the tube, lowering the fundamental pitch.

Velum—A "curtain" that hangs down from the soft palate. It affects vocal nasality.

Vibrato—A periodic change in pitch, intensity or timbre, occurring at a rate of around 5 to 7 pulsations per second. The vibrato is considered a musical ornament, increasing the beauty in the tone. It also changes the quality of the tone psychologically.

Viscera—Organs located in the abdominal cavity.

Vital capacity—The total volume of air that can be inspired and/or expired.

Voiced consonants—Those consonants requiring phonation.

Volley theory—To account for the re-charging time of the auditory nerve before it is capable of being fired again, it is assumed that the nerves fire alternately. A volley of fire.

Vowel and diphthong—A vocal sound produced without occluding, diverting, or obstructing the flow of air from the lungs (as opposed to consonants). Diphthongs are a combination of two vowel sounds as in the word "beautiful," ee-oo.

Wavelength—The distance between any point on a wave to the corresponding point in the next cycle.

Waveshape—The variation in air pressure of a sound, as seen on the oscilloscope. The waveshape provides an exact, scientific graph of tone quality.

White noise—Noise, with most of its acoustical energy lying in the high frequency range.